Application Servers

Powering the Web-Based Enterprise

Application Servers

Powering the Web-Based Enterprise

Jesse Feiler

Morgan Kaufmann

AN IMPRINT OF ACADEMIC PRESS
A Harcourt Science and Technology Company

San Diego San Francisco New York Boston
London Sydney Tokyo

ACADEMIC PRESS
A Harcourt Science and Technology Company
525 B Street, Suite 1900, San Diego, CA 92101-4495 USA
http://www.academicpress.com

Academic Press
24-28 Oval Road, London NW1 7DX United Kingdom
http://www.hbuk.co.uk/ap/

Morgan Kaufmann Publishers
340 Pine Street, Sixth Floor, San Francisco, CA 94104-3205 USA
http://www.mkp.com

Library of Congress Catalog Number: 99-067288

ISBN: 0-12-251338-X

Printed in the United States of America
99 00 01 02 03 IP 6 5 4 3 2 1

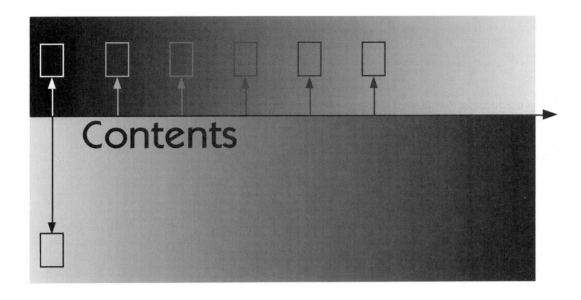

Contents

Introduction   I

Part I. Design   7

Chapter 1. The World of Application Servers   9

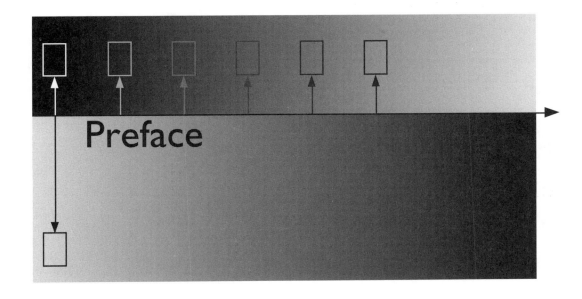

Preface

This book is about one of the most important aspects of the powerful Web sites that organizations large and small now depend on: application servers. As you will see, the definition of an application server varies from vendor to vendor. However, the schematic diagrams from each of those vendors make clear that they all are addressing the same issue in the same way: only the names and the packaging differ.

The functionality that application servers provide is not new: as you will see, the original proposal for the World Wide Web (written in 1989) includes the functionality of an application server. It is only with the dramatic increase in dynamically generated Web pages and the phenomenal growth of e-commerce that application servers have *achieved their current highly visible position among tools that make today's Web possible.*

Who Should Read This Book

This book is geared to IT professionals who are familiar with some of the underlying technologies (Internet, Web, databases, or traditional system design). If you are not familiar with those technologies, the companion book, *Database-Driven Web Sites,* provides a good grounding in the basics. If you are proficient in all of those technologies, you are well-prepared to use application servers.

If, however, you are more comfortable with traditional system technologies (databases, for example) than you are with Internet technologies—or, if you are more comfortable with Web technologies than you are with traditional system design (such as transactional processing)—then this book will bring you up to speed on all of the necessary technology.

It is also addressed to Webmasters and others who are pushing the limits of HTML and other authoring tools and who need to interact with corporate databases and traditional IT applications.

Application Servers: The State of the Art

Application servers bring together a variety of existing technologies in an architecture whose roots go back a number of decades in the computing world. Studies and analyses repeatedly have shown that information technology (IT) professionals believe that application servers are one of the most—if not the most—important developments in the field today. Individual application servers are evolving each day: this evolution takes the form not only of changes to each application server's technology and strategic focus but also the form of mergers and acquistions. Sometimes, a change in corporate structure produces a corporation with two application servers that need to be merged in some way (as is the case with Sun Microsystems and Netscape); in other cases, a company purchases an application server or a key piece of technology as a way of getting a leg up on the market.

The appendix of this book provides a run-down of major application servers. This list is subject to change as application servers themselves change—in name, owner, and features. You will find updated information from the appendix of the book on the author's Web site at http://www.philmont-mill.com. (Click on the Application Servers tab.)

Precisely because the underpinning of application servers are fairly well defined (although the application servers are still in a state of flux), you can do your homework by reading this book in preparation for selecting and using an application server that may not even be on the market at this time. In a sense, the information in the body of this book serves as footnotes to the information provided in the appendix.

The Terminology of Application Servers	Application servers have evolved in the rapidly changing world of the Web in the 1990s. For those who have been there—and been interested in the technologies—application servers are a relatively simple compendium of the technologies that are in daily use throughout the Web. However, for people who either have not followed the Web technologies closely or who have focused only on the areas that impact them, the world of application servers presents a host of acronyms that can be daunting.

This book focuses on the principles that make application servers possible and the technologies that they use. How much you need to know about IIOP (Internet Inter-ORB Protocol) to use an application server is up to you; this book will let you know what it is and provide you with the basics that will often be sufficient for you to understand the issues and to move on to the next acronym.

This book serves as an overview of contemporary computer issues ranging from object technology and component software to database connectivity and usability design.

The Language of Application Servers	Application servers are not wedded to a single language, database, or object model; however, there are many people who believe—and will loudly state—that application servers are Java creatures. Indeed, IBM's description of its WebSphere Application Server describes it as a "Java servlet engine" to be used in conjunction with a variety of HTTP servers. Microsoft, on the other hand, places little emphasis on Java—and even less on application servers, declaring that its Windows NT operating system *is* its application server product.

In point of fact, these discussions have more to do with marketing than with technology (although there are very significant technological issues involved in choosing one language or architecture over another). The principles of application servers are not tied to a single language, database, or object model. Nevertheless, the current lay of the land has a very large number of application server products using Java and the CORBA object model. If this book is too Java-oriented (or too COM-oriented, which it may be for the CORBA purist), remember that its focus is application servers.

How the Book Is Organized

The book is organized around the phases of development and deployment of computer systems: design, development, production, and maintenance. The final part of the book describes a variety of application servers.

Part I: Design	This part of the book details the architecture and design of application servers and the world in which they live. This is a world that is centered on the Internet; it includes modern programming techniques and principles including databases and component software.
The World of Application Servers	The world of application servers is the world of the Internet. Even if application servers are deployed on internal networks, they frequently use Internet technology either in whole or in part. The world of the Internet is a world of internationally recognized standards—and of rapid changes. This chapter provides an overview.
Application Servers Today	What exactly are application servers? This chapter provides a roadmap to the functionalities that they provide. It also includes a comparison of a variety of application servers. In this high-stakes field that is full of innovation and mutation, it should come as no surprise that each vendor has a different perspective on what application servers are—and aren't.
Databases and Application Servers	Application servers almost always work in conjunction with databases. In this chapter you will find an overview of databases as they exist today.
Sub-Programs and Application Servers	Applets, plug-ins, user procedures, and other code modules are used to extend and enhance Web servers and browsers,

	databases, and even application servers. This chapter provides a brief overview of this architecture.
Components, Objects, and Application Servers	Component software—software using designs such as COM and CORBA—is an integral part of application servers and their environment. From components to plug-ins, this chapter surveys the world of software below the program level.

Part II: Development	Building on the designs and architectures described in Part I, this part of the book shows you how to use application servers.
Developing the Interface	Applets, ActiveX controls, and JavaBeans are technologies that let you enhance the interface for users. They run in the user's browser and can enliven the interface; more importantly, they can serve as an interface to application servers.
Connecting to Logic: COM, CORBA, EJB, and RMI	Components are a critical part of today's software development environment. This chapter builds on the design issues described in Part I showing you how to actually use widely available component technologies (such as JavaBeans) with application servers.
Connecting to Data: ODBC and JDBC	The connections between application servers and databases are often implemented using ODBC and JDBC technologies. They are described in this chapter.

Part III: Production	Once a system has been designed and developed, it moves into production. The world in which application servers actually run is a very complex world.

Transaction Processing and TP Monitors	This chapter explores the issues involved in handling transactions (such as e-commerce sales).
Security and Application Servers	Security is a complex and critical issue not only for e-commerce but also for sites that "merely" provide information. Dangers can arise from malevolent intruders as well as from accidents. This chapters shows you what can happen and what you can do to minimize problems.
Small-Scale Application Servers	Application servers are used to run enormous e-commerce sites; they also can be used to run very small sites. This chapter provides an overview of small-scale application servers including those that can be implemented on a single personal computer.

Part IV: Maintenance	This part of the book focuses on maintenance: the routine and exceptional tasks that you need to carry out to keep your application server and its Web site functioning properly.
Designing for Maintenance	This chapter builds on the previous chapters that have addressed maintenance. In those, you saw how to design for the developers who will be modifying your code later on as well as how to factor maintenance into production. There is more, however. In this chapter, you will see how you need to design for maintenance even in the user interface—so that your users will be able to participate in keeping your site current.
Managing Feedback	Application servers help you open up your organization to large numbers of people—customers, employees, the media, and critics. How do you handle this increased visibility? Mimeographed form letters do not apply in this world. This chapter addresses these issues.

How To Get There From Here	The last chapter in this part of the book provides a roadmap for moving toward Web-based enterprises powered by application servers.
Appendix: Application Servers Today	The appendix provides information about many of the application servers on the market today. This information has been provided by the vendors of the various products, and it represents the status and features of their products as this book has gone to press. Updates to the appendix can be found on the Web at http://www.philmontmill.com.

Related Books

Database-Driven Web Sites and *Managing the Web-Based Enterprise* both provide additional perspectives on the material covered in this book. The first provides an overview of the Internet and the Web as well as a detailed look at the use of databases on modern Web sites. The second focuses on the issues involved in integrating the Internet in general and the Web in particular to existing (and new) organizations. Both are published by Morgan Kaufmann.

For More Information...

You can find further information on this topic (together with updates to the book and information on the books mentioned in the previous section) on the author's Web site. It is located at http://www.philmontmill.com.

Acknowledgements

Carole McClendon of Waterside Productions has made this project—like so many others—go smoothly.

Ken Morton has the author's heartfelt thanks for helping to bring this series of three books to fruition. As before, Julie Bolduc, senior production editor, has once again made the process of actually producing the book as painless as possible. Finally, Gary Ragaglia has designed an attractive and eye-catching cover.

This book was written and produced on Macintosh computers using Adobe FrameMaker. Other products used include Adobe Photoshop, FileMaker Pro, Flash-It, FreeHand, Microsoft Word, Microsoft Windows, Virtual PC, Microsoft Access, and AppleWorks.

Despite the help and assistance from so many people, any errors remain the author's.

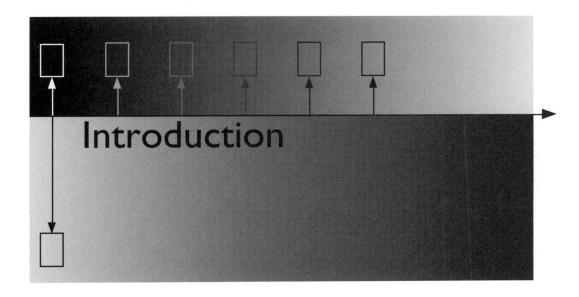

Introduction

Application servers are not new: they have been part of the design of the World Wide Web from the start. Like the Web itself—which was then called an Information Mesh—application servers did not get their name until later.

Application servers are a critical part of the evolving world of dynamic Web sites and e-commerce. Their functionality is necessary in order to keep today's Web operating properly. Each major vendor of Internet software has an application server (or two!) in their catalog of software, although some vendors call application servers by other names.

A Short History of the Computer Age

The designers of the earliest computers were aiming for computation engines to compute logarithmic tables, ballistic trajectories, astronomical orbits, code-breaking algorithms, and long-range weather forecasts.

However, if you look back at the popular impressions of computers in the 1950s (when the idea of a computer was taking shape), you will find that computers were imagined to be primarily database machines with a little bit of computation thrown in. The idea of large databases ("data banks") really took hold in the popular imagination.

In fact, over the decades, it is a third aspect of computers that has proven to be the most potent force for change: telecommunications. Computers today make possible the global telecommunications network, but more importantly computers today facilitate communications between and among individuals and organizations, carrying large amounts of data to and fro around the globe.

In this book, you will frequently see references to a three-part system architecture: one part is the user interface and comomunications (often a Web server), another part is a database, and the intermediate part is an application server—a computational engine that connects the two. These three parts correspond exactly to these three major aspects of the computer age: computation, data storage, and communications.

The Origin of Application Servers

Application servers are described in Tim Berners-Lee's initial proposal for the World Wide Web[1]. The phrase was not applied to them until later—and in the case of Microsoft, the phrase is rarely used even today.

Figure I-1 is reproduced from the original proposal for the Web (then called an Information Mesh). In the lower left, the Hypertext Server provides the Generic Browser with hypertext-based content—today's HTML. In the lower right, the "dummy Hypertext server" takes data from a database and makes it look like Hypertext to the browser.

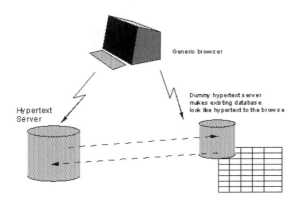

___

FIGURE I-1. Original Proposal for the World Wide Web: Figure 3.

That—and more—is what application servers do today. The important point to note is that the user sitting at the Generic Browser cannot tell the difference between Hypertext coming from a Hypertext server (in modern terms, pages coded in HTML) and Hypertext coming from a database and automatically transformed into that format.

___

1. You can find the original document on the Web. Its URL is http://www.w3.org/History/1989/proposal.html.

Today, the Web has moved beyond hypertext and even hypermedia to embrace transactions (such as e-commerce) that were definitely not part of the original design. However, the role of application servers on the Web is old news.

What Does "Application" Mean?

Although the basic functionality of application servers is clear—they do what they were shown to be doing in the original Web designs—terminology is sometimes confusing. In fact, even the word "application" has great ambiguity. In some ways, it is like "nice" and "bad"—words whose meanings have reversed over time. ("Cleave" is an even more extreme case: in modern usage it has two diametrically opposed meanings.)

"Application" is used in two ways today:

1. In organizations with IT staffs, "application" is frequently used to refer to an operation such as payroll or inventory that is carried out through the use of one or more computer systems.

2. In the world of personal computers, "application" is frequently used to refer to application programs—individual programs that are used for a variety of purposes. In this usage, a word processing program—whether used for employee evaluations or creating advertising materials—is an application. Application software in this sense is distinguished from system software—operating systems and the like.

Application servers are involved with applications in the first sense—an organization's operations that involve a variety of systems.

What Is a Web-Based Enterprise?

Application servers power Web-based enterprises, but what are Web-based enterprises? Here are a few characteristics of the organizations that use—or are likely to use—application servers.

- Enterprises are often large, but they need not be. They may be for-profit companies, non-profit organizations (non-governmental organizations), or governmental entities.

- They use Internet technology—particularly the World Wide Web—to carry out their operations.

- They frequently are global in scope; if not global, they very often are distributed among several locations.

- They have reevaluated their operations within the last decade.

Do You Need an Application Server?

Application servers are necessary to support Web sites that use dynamic data—data that is prepared as needed from one or more databases, from template files, from scripts, and from user input. Such sites range from e-commerce sites with their catalogs and shopping carts to libraries of information that is prepared on demand.

Application servers are integrated with some database products; desktop software such as Microsoft Access and FileMaker Pro provide application server functionality (although the name is not used). High-end databases also provide application server functionality—most often as an additional product.

What Do You Need to Use an Application Server?

An application server works in conjunction with a Web server such as Apache or Microsoft Internet Information Server. The Web server manages the interaction with users across the Internet while the application server provides the formatted information to be delivered to those users.

An application server is often located close to the Web server—often on the same computer. Smaller organizations may use the Web and application servers at their Internet Service Providers (ISPs). Sometimes the application server is integrated with the Web server; other times it is separate.

Product, Methodology, or Architecture?

Application servers are products in many cases. In other cases, however, the concept of application servers seems more like a methodology for developing and deploying systems or like an architecture for their design. Each notion of application servers is correct in its own way.

The basic architecture of application servers—the separation of user interface from data management and from business logic in between—is an architecture that has appeared many times over the last decades. In a recent incarnation it has appeared as client/server or multi/tier architectures.

Keep in mind these different uses of the term. If you believe that going out and buying something called an "application server" will solve all your problems, it will not. Understanding how application servers—as products, methodology, or architecture—fit into your world is a useful and productive endeavor.

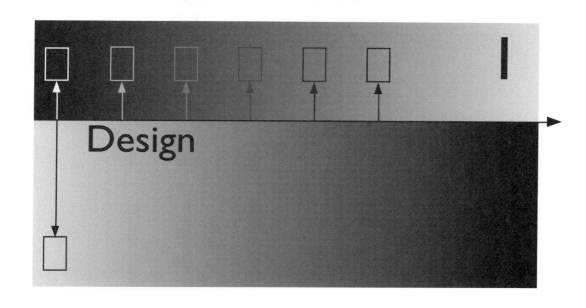

Design

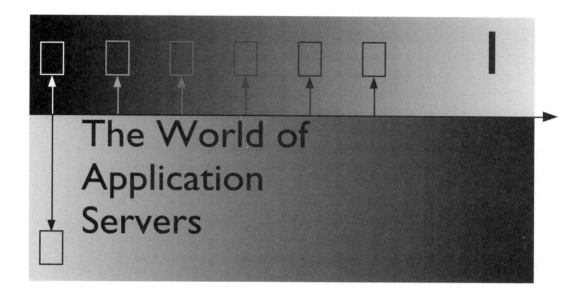

The World of Application Servers

This part of the book details the architecture and design of application servers and the world in which they live. This is a world that is centered on the Internet; it includes modern programming techniques and principles including databases and component software.

This chapter explores the environment in which application servers function. While you can find application servers used in a small application written for use on a single desktop computer, more often they are deployed across the Internet as part of enterprise-wide systems. They often interact with legacy systems—computer systems that are years (and sometimes decades) old. Furthermore, they often are part of far-flung endeavors that are global in scope.

Knowing the world of application servers helps you appreciate the types of problems that they have been designed to solve and to understand the terminology that is used. You need not limit your uses of application servers to these problems, and you may choose to use different terminology for your projects; however, it is important not to reinvent the wheel. Precisely because application servers exist at the intersection of large corporate information systems, personal computers, and the Internet, it is very easy to inadvertently duplicate effort and to foster misunderstandings.

Thus, this chapter focuses on these critical aspects of the world of application servers:

- *The Internet,*

- *Software architecture today,*

- *Enterprise computing,*

- *Legacy systems, and*

- *Globalization.*

It is important to note that databases are also an integral part of the world of application servers. However, they are so important that they are not covered in this chapter—you will find them discussed in Chapter 3, "Databases and Application Servers" starting on page 55.

The Internet

The Internet is more than three decades old, but for many people it is quite a recent phenomenon. For them, the Internet is the World Wide Web—and the Web is barely ten years old. In fact, the Web is only part of the Internet (albeit the most visible part).

The Internet is actually quite simple. Its protocols, conventions, and standards are not hard for even a novice programmer to understand; in fact, at several times in the evolution of the Internet, more complex versions of protocols, conventions, and standards have been passed over in favor of simpler ones.

Much of the popularity of the Internet stems from this simplicity: its scope and complexity are functions of the simplicity of its design and its ability to be implemented and reimplemented on a grand scale.

There are many books and articles on the Internet[1]; this section touches on the issues that are most relevant to application servers and the uses to which they are put.

The Internet itself is basically a set of protocols and other agreements that allow messages to be transferred quickly among computers that can be located anywhere in the world. There really are only three relevant issues:

1. The protocols for transferring messages.

2. The conventions for addressing messages.

3. The formats of those messages.

Transfer Protocols

There are two sets of transfer protocols that are important on the Internet. These protocols have evolved over the years through the work of committees. Requests for Comments (RFCs) are circulated electronically and they gradually evolve into the standards that are in use. RFCs are numbered, and you can find them in various places on the Internet. (Use a search engine to search on RFC to find them.)

---

1. The material in this section is dealt with at much greater length in *Database-Driven Web Sites*.

TCP/IP

The first deals with the transmissions of messages—any messages. It is called Transmission Control Protocol/Internet Protocol (TCP/IP).

Functional Protocols

The second set of transfer protocols deal with specific functions or applications. The Hypertext Transfer Protocol (HTTP) supports Web pages; the File Transfer Protocol (FTP) supports transfer of files between computers; the Telnet protocol supports remote use of computers over the Internet; and a variety of other protocols support e-mail (these include Simple Mail Transfer Protocol—SMTP and Post Office Protocol—POP).

Addressing Conventions

Every device on the Internet is addressable. In fact, the addressing mechanism is part of the TCP/IP protocol, but in practice you will need to deal with address issues much more than with the basic telecommunication issues addressed by TCP/IP. Internet addressing conventions involve numeric IP addresses and more readable domain names.

IP Addresses

Every device on the Internet has an IP (Internet Protocol) address. That address consists of a quartet of numbers, such as 198.162.1.1, 205.231.14.2, and so forth. The numbers have significance and are in a way very much like telephone numbers where the first group of digits specifies a country code, the second group specifies an area code within the country, the third group specifies a local exchange, and the final group specifies the individual line.

A numbering scheme like this means that new numbers can be assigned without having recourse to any central authority: when you apply for a new telephone number, your local telephone company (which owns the exchange) can assign the number to you. Likewise, within a single country's code, new area codes can be defined at any time since they cannot interfere with those in another country.

Domain Name System

You sometimes use an IP address—the quartet of numbers—to get to a Web site. More often, though, you use a domain name—such as www.abc.com. Domain names are read from right to left. The right-most component (com, in this example) is called a root. Roots include com (commercial), edu (education), and net (network) in the United States; other roots are beginning to appear. In other countries, the root identifies the country (uk for United Kingdom, il for Israel, and so forth).

Since the actual communications on the Internet involve numeric IP addresses, it is necessary to convert these domain names to the appropriate IP address. This is done automatically by domain name servers throughout the Internet. Each root (com, edu, il, uk, and so forth) has its own root server. In response to queries from around the Internet, it provides the IP addresses for the domains within it—that is, for the domains with the root name and with one name to the left. Thus, the root server for com will provide IP addresses for abc.com, def.com, and so forth.

Those IP addresses represent the IP addresses of domain name servers—servers that can recursively provide IP addresses within the domain. A domain name server for abc.com is responsible for providing the actual IP address for www.abc.com (as well as for any other addresses, such as shopping.abc.com, www.database.abc.com, and so forth).

As you can see, this mechanism is highly distributed; it is implemented with caching on many servers. With caching, a server that has recently gotten an IP address for a domain can continue to use that address without bothering to query the root or the domain again. (Rules for caching are provided as part of the Internet's domain name system protocols.)

A domain name server is normally associated with your Internet connection: it functions in a complementary manner. It is usually located at your Internet service provider (ISP), and it keeps track of domain names within your Internet service provider as well as of the IP addresses of root servers. In this way, you can get to root servers in order to get information about their subdomains. Your local domain name server usually keeps a cache of the IP addresses that it has obtained recently. This speeds processing for people who access the same domain frequently.

What It Means to You

Using domain names is much easier for most people than using IP addresses. It also makes it easier to move computers around. You may move your domain from one computer to another—even from one Internet service provider to another, but if you are asking people to use your domain name, they will never know about the change. The Internet's domain name system will handle this.

In practice, it often takes a day for these changes to ripple through the Internet. During that time, different people may get different results when they type in your domain name.

Typically, updates to this information are done overnight, so many people find it useful to implement a domain name or IP address change on a Saturday night; this provides two nights and a fairly slow day (in the business world) for changes to propagate through the Internet.

Note also that changes to IP addresses within your domain need to be managed at the level of your domain name server. You do not need to update your main domain registration record (at the root server) unless the address of your domain name server changes.

You normally do not deal with a root server: you do, however, deal with an Internet registration service when you register your domain name. That registration includes updating of the root server.

Message Formats

The third issue of Internet design that you need to consider is the standard message formats. These are the formats of the messages that are sent via the various transfer protocols (FTP, HTTP, and so forth).

Transfer Formats Versus Message Formats

Some of the transfer protocols—such as FTP—have no message formats. You can transfer a file from one computer to another over the Internet, and only you and the recipient need to agree on its internal format. (That is why transferring files from a Windows computer to a Unix computer may not succeed.)

Other formats, however, like the mail formats and the Web format—HTML (Hypertext Markup Language), are specified to allow you to transfer content without worrying about the format. This is how you can use the mail formats (such as SMTP and POP) to transfer mail messages with embedded text styling: you use either HTML or the MIME (Multipart Internet Message Exchange) protocol to send and receive a universally recognized format.

Why This Matters

In the world of application servers, you rely on the HTML format to send and receive data. The application server generates HTML as needed, often converting proprietary database formats into standard HTML. Likewise, the application server pulls user-specified information out of HTML and sends it to databases and other applications.

Although application servers need not use HTML (and need not even use the Internet), from a practical point of view, they use the Internet and HTML to accomplish their work.

Putting It Together

Figure 1-1 provides a schematic view of the Internet. A user at a personal computer (in the lower left) connects—often via phone or cable—to an Internet service provider. This connection—like all of the connections in the diagram—is both physical and logical.

Physically, it may consist of telephone wires, cable television media, or wireless communications. However, once the link has been established, the communication between you and your ISP is via TCP/IP. And, over that TCP/IP communications link, other message protocols for mail, Internet news, the Web, and so forth, can be transmitted.

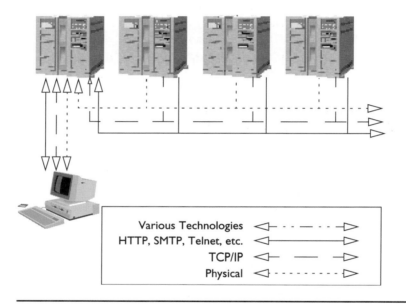

FIGURE 1-1. Internet Design

The communications between other computers on the Internet are similar. There are physical connections linking individual computers, but the TCP/IP protocol is what serves the users: they rarely if ever need to be concerned about the physical connection. (Remember that addresses are technically part of the TCP/IP protocol, not part of the physical connection.)

At an even higher or more abstract level, communications between Web server and Web user use the HTTP protocol; neither is concerned with either the physical connection or the TCP/IP connection.

The Internet service provider connects via TCP/IP to other computers throughout the Internet. It provides a domain name server to resolve your requests for various domains and to convert them into numeric IP addresses. The computers to which you connect via TCP/IP may be located in the same location as your Internet service provider, or they may be located around the world. None of this matters once you have made the connection to the Internet.

Software Architecture Today

Software has evolved tremendously since the dawn of the computer age half a century ago. That evolution has made the world of application servers possible. The critical aspects that impinge on application servers are:

- Evolution of software design,

- Evolution of interaction design,

- Contemporary system design on the Internet, and

- Beyond the Internet—where application servers come into play.

Evolution of Software Design

Until the late 1980s, software architecture typically looked more or less like the schematic diagram shown in Figure 1-2. The user interacted with a monolithic program that contained code to manage the application, its data, the user interface, and communications.

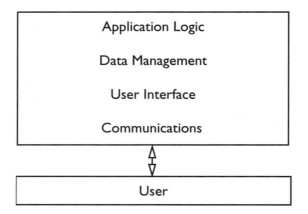

FIGURE 1-2. Software Functionality

In fact, until fairly recently, those functionalities were jumbled together much as they are in Figure 1-3. (Should you find yourself stymied over a programming problem, you can attempt to unscramble the letters in Figure 1-3 into the words in Figure 1-2. One letter is missing.)

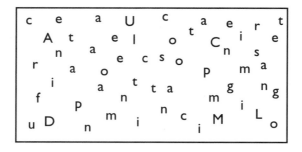

FIGURE 1-3. Primordial Software Design

A great step forward in programming design in the 1970s was the introduction of structured programming: an architecture that converted the primordial design of Figure 1-3 into the more logical design of Figure 1-2. Once the inherent logic of a program had been revealed by structuring its functions, people began to move to the next step: questioning why those functions needed to be written and rewritten in every program. The structure made clear that communications for a payroll program were essentially the same as those for a rocket trajectory calculator. And, when both communications functions used the same protocols (as in the Internet), writing duplicative code became even more and more questionable.

Evolution of Interaction Design	Meanwhile, a similar evolution was taking place in the field of interaction design: how the user interacts with computers. This evolution had three main phases:

1. Dumb terminal systems,

2. Client/server systems, and

3. Internet client/server systems.

Dumb Terminal Systems	Initially, the terminals that people used to interact with computers were dumb: they displayed text and allowed for the entry of text. Teletypes and cathode ray tube-based monitors were typical of these terminals. Figure 1-4 shows how programs were designed to use these terminals.

The user's interaction is with the remote computer. It runs an operating system which runs the application, communications software, and data management. During the 1970s, communications software and data management gradually were removed from individual applications, following the logic in the previous section (they did not need to be reinvented for each application). However, each new application did need to implement its own interface.

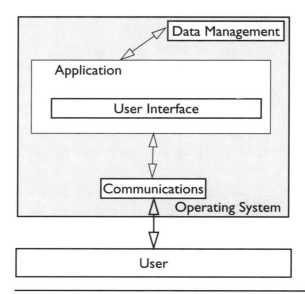

FIGURE 1-4. Dumb Terminal Design

Client/Server Systems

With the advent of personal computers, dumb terminals were gradually replaced with personal computers. Processing was shared between the remote computer (the server) and the local personal computer (the client), as shown in Figure 1-5.

A communication link was established between software running on the client and on the server; via this link, the user interface and data display/preparation software on each computer could communicate.

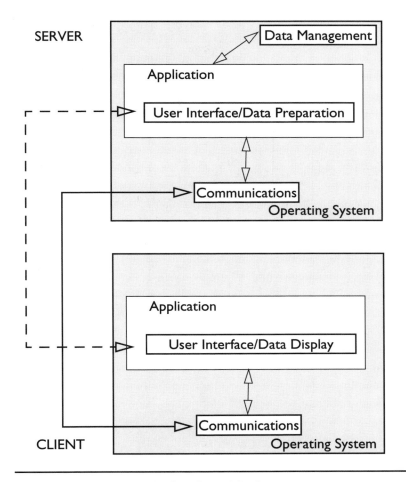

FIGURE 1-5. Smart Terminal (Client/Server) Design

Internet Client/ Server Systems

Figure 1-6 provides some renaming of Figure 1-5; otherwise it is the same.

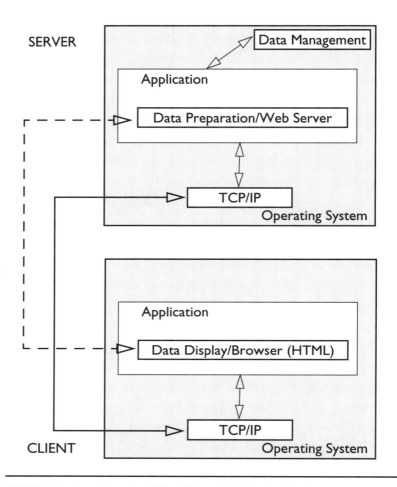

FIGURE 1-6. Smart Terminal (Client/Server) Design for the Internet

This really is just another perspective of the first figure in this chapter (Figure 1-1 in "Putting It Together" starting on page 15). TCP/IP communications software on client and server systems interacts to provide a communications link; data display on the client is provided using HTML and a standard display product—an Internet browser. The process of preparing data on the server is done by standard Web server software. The use of so much standard software means that implementing a system can be done very easily: only the new logic specific to the application needs to be coded.

There are additional protocols and interfaces in use today; some are custom-written while others reflect the use of the Internet as an integral part of modern computing. For example, Microsoft Office2000 allows users to collaborate on Word documents over the Web without using HTML or a browser.

Contemporary System Design on the Internet

Figure 1-7 shows this architecture again; this time the role of the application server is included. The diagram includes images of the client and server computers (at left); each contains all of the functionality shown in the box to its right.

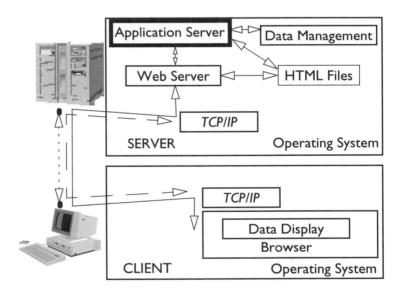

FIGURE 1-7. Internet Terminology for Client/Server

As you can see, the client computer relies on TCP/IP and a browser to display the data and interact with the user and server. In many cases, no additional software is needed (this is what is often referred to as a thin client). This has tremendous benefits not only in the development of new applications but also in their deployment: there is nothing to install and nothing to update on the client computer.

On the server side, TCP/IP maintains communications, and a standard Web server interacts with the user's browser on the client side. A new piece of software—the application server—interacts with a database and with HTML file templates. Whereas a Web server typically simply returns static HTML files, the application server combines templates, data from the data base, and other elements to dynamically create HTML files for the Web server to download. The Web server may not be aware that it is downloading anything other than a text-based HTML file.

In this architecture, a new system can typically be implemented by writing code for the application server and writing some new HTML template files. Nothing else needs to be touched.

Note that this architecture is sometimes modified in practice. A given vendor may provide a product that combines two or more of the elements shown in Figure 1-7. Microsoft Internet Information Server, for example, combines the Web server and application server functionalities. FileMaker Web Companion combines the data management and application server functionalities. Other products from other vendors do similar things—for reasons of design as well as of marketing.

This architecture allows for fast implementation of new systems; however, not every system is new, and not every system easily falls into this architecture. As a result, yet another extension to the architecture is sometimes provided.

Beyond the Internet

Figure 1-8 shows the final extension of the architecture of Figure 1-7. Each computer in this diagram should be assumed to contain all of the functionality shown in Figure 1-7 (the omission is simply to make the diagram a little less cluttered).

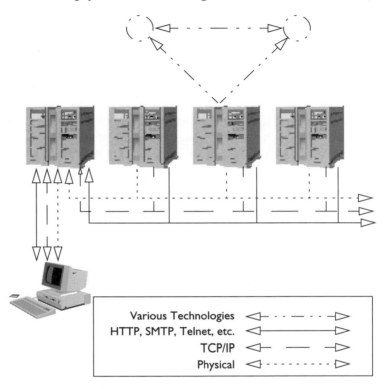

Various Technologies

HTTP, SMTP, Telnet, etc.

TCP/IP

Physical

FIGURE 1-8. Integrated Internet, Legacy, and Other Systems

Note at the top that one of the computers uses various communication technologies to communicate with other computers and processes. These are not (necessarily) Internet communication technologies, and the protocols involved may be private and idiosyncratic. However, when they are returned to the computer, its application server software converts them to the standard Internet protocols, and in that way they can be sent out across the Internet. It is in this way that non-Internet systems can be drawn into Internet-based applications.

Non-Internet Connectivity	Notwithstanding the widespread use of the Internet, it is not used for all communications between and among computers. Dumb terminals are still in use in many environments, and protocols other than TCP/IP are common in many installations. Application servers (particularly standalone application servers) often support protocols other than TCP/IP and the Web. This allows legacy systems and legacy hardware to be integrated into the latest technology.
Application Hosting	Application hosting refers to the environment in which an application (such as payroll, inventory management, or other business operations) is hosted at a remote site and accessed via Internet protocols. While this architecture has certain features in common with application servers, it is less a distinct architecture than an implementation of standard systems using Internet protocols.

Enterprise Computing

The environment of application servers often is that of the enterprise—a large organization that is frequently dispersed over a wide area. Enterprises normally have information technology (IT) staffs—either on payroll or as consultants. They typically maintain their own Internet connections, using commercial ISPs for backup purposes. (They may use enterprise-oriented ISPs for their networking, but those are typically different ISPs than the ones you contract with for personal Internet access.)

The existence of IT staffs is very important in enterprise computing: it means that resources are available in-house to solve problems and to maintain systems. In addition, enterprise computing normally means that large systems (both business systems and computer systems) come into play.

In addition, enterprise computing often involves legacy systems.

Legacy Systems

Legacy systems are those systems that are running—often well—and have been running for years (and sometimes for decades). They have typically been maintained (more or less) and patched over time; their original designers may not even recognize them.

They often use hardware and software that is not current and that cannot be replaced. Why, you may wonder, are they still around? The answers are simple.

Legacy Systems Are Paid For

Legacy systems are old—and paid for. Their costs have been amortized over time, and their cost is only that of maintenance.

This is a typical problem for business planners: a large investment in new technology or facilities may be a good long-term investment, but often a business's performance is judged on short-term results. Software and hardware are no different from other investments.

The Cost of Replacement Is High	The cost of replacing legacy systems is high—and it only starts with the cost of the system itself. The cost of data conversion can be substantial, and the cost of retraining users can be very significant. Furthermore, there is normally more risk involved in replacing a system than in incrementally repairing it.
Repair Is Faster Than Replacement	In addition to the absolute cost, repairs are almost always faster than replacement of systems. Computer systems—perhaps more than other technologies—are often run until they can run no more.
	One method that is sometimes used to attempt to get the best of both worlds is to do partial upgrades and replacements: the architecture of a legacy system may be retained, but a significant portion—such as the user interface—is converted to a new technology (such as client/server or Internet client/server).
Bridges Can Be Built	Finally, legacy software tends to stay around in enterprises because the existence of a trained IT staff—including people familiar with the legacy systems—means that it is feasible to build bridges between the legacy systems and new systems. (This is a variant on the partial replacement discussed in the previous section.)
	In fact, Figure 1-8 can be interpreted as showing bridges between the Internet world and two legacy systems (at the top of the diagram).
	A critical part of the bridges between Internet client/server systems and legacy systems can be application servers. Many application servers, in fact, are designed primarily as bridges.

(Products from major database vendors such as IBM and Oracle fall squarely into this camp.)

Globalization

Today's globalization (as opposed to that of previous eras) is made possible by very cheap and fast telecommunications—in other words, the Internet and its technologies. Thomas L. Friedman's definition is among the best:

> ...globalization involves the inexorable integration of markets, nation-states, and technologies to a degree never witnessed before—in a way that is enabling individuals, corporations, and nation-states to reach around the world farther, faster, deeper and cheaper than ever before...[2]

What, you may wonder, does this have to do with application servers? To the extent that the Internet is a major factor in today's globalization, and to the extent that application servers have a critical role to play in making the Internet available to enterprises and their computer systems, they play a critical role. An enterprise's legacy systems are almost always remnants of the Cold War age—the age before globalization. Communications were neither as cheap or fast as they are today; expectations of performance for computer systems were much lower.

Furthermore, one of the major aspects of today's globalization—the rapid spread of technology and its resources to people around the world—was not present in the previous age. Companies could—and did—thrive on being data fortresses: you had to go to them (hat in hand) to get the information that you needed. You needed to negotiate with intermediaries—

---

2. *The Lexus and the Olive Tree*, Thomas L. Friedman, Farrar Straus & Giroux, New York, 1999, p. 7.

often several—in order to gain access to the hallowed halls and to find your way around.

Today, companies thrive on being data warehouses—serve-yourself warehouses where the goods are stacked floor to ceiling and the sales personnel are nowhere to be found (they're surfing the Net searching for new information merchandise).

Organizations around the world are dealing with globalization: converting to this new age or starting afresh as is the case with new companies. Because application servers can be a key to integrating legacy systems with this new world, you need to be aware of the issues involved in globalization: if you repeat the words, "access," "fast," and "do-it-yourself," you will not go far wrong. Building an application server-based system that responds to the environment of the 1960s (or even the 1990s) is no way to get ahead. The world has changed since the walls came down (the Wall in Berlin and the more insidious one that walled people off from information in computers controlled by mysterious others).

Summary

This chapter has dealt with five of the most important aspects of the world in which application servers are used:

- The Internet,
- Software architecture today,
- Enterprise computing,
- Legacy systems, and
- Globalization.

The Internet makes it all possible, and today's software architecture makes it possible to use the Internet to disperse functionality among a variety of computers while using standard protocols and formats. Beyond those two technical issues, the world of application servers involves enterprise computing—large companies with IT staffs, legacy systems—the old, but often irreplaceable systems that run major organizations, and globalization—the fast way for people to handle their information tasks themselves.

The next chapter focuses directly on application servers and how they fit into this world.

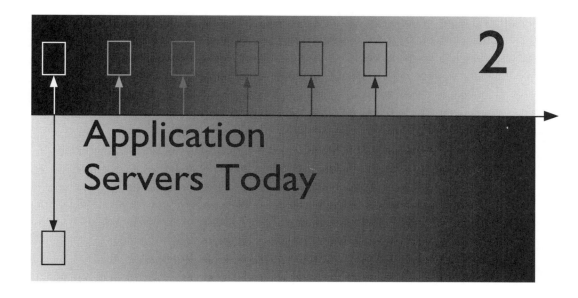

Application Servers Today

The world of the Internet, modern software architecture, enterprise computing, legacy systems, and globalization that was described in the previous chapter plays host to application servers. In this chapter, you will find a general description of what they do and how they do it. It provides a high-level overview of application servers that will be refined and enhanced in later chapters.

For now, the key points that you need to know about application servers are:

- How they are used,

- How they work, and

- The types of application servers.

What Application Servers Do

Application servers typically come into play as part of the answer to questions such as these:

- Can we use the Web to access legacy systems and databases?

- Can we do something to automate our Web site's creation rather than creating each page's HTML by hand?

- Can we build a Web-based system with the same rigorous design and testing standards that we use in other information systems?

- Can we move a PC-based system onto the Web?

- Can we implement an e-commerce solution?

- Can we improve the performance of our (sluggish) Web site?

These questions demonstrate the six classic uses of application servers. It is important to note that pure instances of these uses are rare: in most cases, real-life projects combine a variety of uses. Nevertheless, these paradigms of use can be helpful in understanding the power and scope of application servers.

The basic paradigms of application server use are:

- Integration with Legacy Systems and Databases

- Web Site Support

- Web-Integrated System Development

- Personal Computer System Deployment

- E-Commerce

- Performance Management

Integration with Legacy Systems and Databases	In many organizations, there are often very big investments in legacy systems and in the databases that support them. These systems are often found in global enterprises, but they can also exist in small one- or two-person offices. (In small businesses, the proportional investment in such systems is often greater than it is in global enterprises.)
The Problem	These systems hold the organization's data and operations in tight control. How can this fortress be breached to allow new features to be implemented and new technologies (such as the Web) to be integrated?
The Challenge	The challenges involved in integrated legacy systems and databases with modern technologies such as the Web revolve around the criticality of these systems and the way in which they have been developed and maintained.

Legacy Systems Are Critical   These systems not only are old, but they also often form the core of an organization's information technology infrastructure. They may be fragile and outdated (or robust and modern), but they must work.

Not only do these systems contain an organization's records, it often is the case that an organization's policies and procedures are codified only within the code of a legacy system. While basic operational issues are frequently well known, the exact procedures to be followed for rare and peculiar transactions can often only be discovered by reading the code of an ancient computer system to see what actually would happen (for example, death of an employee while on vacation for which an advance of salary has been issued).

Development and Maintenance of Legacy Systems   These systems have evolved over time, incorporating new features that the organization requires as well as taking advantage of technological advances. It is the nature of these systems—and the organizations that own and manage them—to evolve. Wholesale replacement of enterprise-wide systems is a very difficult, expensive, and time-consuming task; as a result, it does not happen every day.

It is not hard to find software designs that are several decades old still in use in such organizations. (In many cases it is not hard to find remnants of 80-column punched cards embedded in system designs.)

Typically, these systems are managed by information technology professionals. Often their orientation is more focused on mainframe-type applications and batch processing than it is on networked personal computer users. Furthermore, their orientation is frequently towards employees rather than customers or other external users. A culture gap often exists between information technology staffs and personal computer and Web-based staffs.

Where Application Servers Fit In

Application servers can be used to provide a Web-based front end to such systems. They can interact with legacy systems or their support databases. One approach is to keep the legacy system or database as an impregnable entity and to use an application server to simulate traditional interaction. In other words, the application server can interact with Web-based users on one side and with the legacy system or database on the other; in extreme cases, the application server can generate messages that actually appear to the legacy system to come from dumb terminals.

In this way, the new technology of the Web can be wedded to the ancient legacy systems and databases without actually touching those older systems.

Note that a number of application servers (particularly the larger ones) provide older protocols in addition to the Web protocols for communication. Thus, you can connect an existing network of dumb terminals to your application server and have the application server's business logic handle both new and old technologies.

How Else to Do It

A common alternative approach to the integration of legacy systems and databases with the Web is to provide periodic (often daily) downloads of data from the legacy system or database to a new and totally Web-based system. (Such a system may well include an application server. See "Web-Integrated System Development" on page 40.)

This is a common approach, since it guarantees that the legacy system or database is untouched by Web-based development and that the Web-based development need not be influenced by legacy considerations. Unfortunately, this approach results in the duplication (and occasional inconsistency) of data as well as the need to maintain two similar systems—one for the Web and one for traditional users. Such an architecture can proliferate in an organization as entire databases are copied on a routine basis from one system to another.

You can see this for yourself in some online banking systems. The bank's traditional accounting system (legacy code) is the core of its operations. Data is downloaded overnight to a separate system that manages its automated teller network. (Sometimes such a system is shared by a number of banks.) Balances are synchronized at that time between the two systems. Deposits made to the ATM network may—or may not—be posted in real time to the basic accounting system just as deposits made at a bank branch may—or may not—be posted in real time to the ATM system. And just to make things livelier, a third system can exist which manages online banking for Web-based customers. It, too, is synchronized periodically with the basic accounting system.

Such data duplication requires extensive error-checking code to be written; it also requires sophisticated code to be implemented to allow for correction of mistakes and reversals of transactions in one (or two or three) interrelated systems. Over time, the cost of maintaining multiple systems almost always exceeds the cost of developing and maintaining a single well-integrated system. Of course, that time period can be long—much longer than most organizations' planning cycles.

Another problem with data duplication—particularly when Web access for customers and other users is allowed—is that people can see and be mystified by inconsistencies in the databases. Depending on the application, this can be an annoyance or a severe problem.

Web Site Support

Individuals and organizations today have Web sites; they are considered a normal part of business and everyday life. (In fact, they are more than everyday life: Web sites exist for people and pets—both living and dead.) Developing and maintaining these sites is a major challenge.

The Problem

In the 1980s, analysts identified a programming backlog that was many years long. Given the amount of time it took to develop and test a system together with the number of systems already requested, new systems appeared to have no chance of seeing the light of day for years—possibly decadees.

OutdJavaBeansated Sites Today, a similar backlog has emerged on the Web. You probably have encountered many Web sites with "current news" listings that are months (or years!) old. Calendars of important events end far in the past. "Future" events on the Web site may be your own distant memories by the time you browse the site.

Complex Sites A small business site can easily run to over a thousand HTML pages. By the time pages have been developed that include press releases, biographies of principal company officials, job openings, descriptions of goods and services, and all of the other necessary information, it is hard to make sense of the site—much less develop and maintain it.

The Challenge

In many organizations, Web sites have grown rapidly. Their origins frequently were in graphics departments, publicity organizations, or informal projects done with minimal management supervision and support. As they become critical parts of organizations, they need more formal supervision and the resources of the mainstream information technology staff that is experienced at handling large amounts of information.

Where Application Servers Fit In

Application servers can be used to power dynamic Web pages such as Active Server Pages (ASP), pages formatted dynamically using Cold Fusion, and other pages that are constructed automatically as needed. Almost all application servers have the ability to combine information from databases and legacy systems with template files, filling placeholders in the template files with relevant information.

Such a structure can be devised even in the absence of legacy systems and databases. You can create a handful of template pages with placeholders for information; you can then create records in a databases that are retrieved as needed for those template pages. The ad hoc nature of the queries can be user driven (such as, "Find all articles about gray cats") but they can also be specified by the Web site designer (such as, "Find all articles dated today"). Updating the database with appropriate information can be done easily by using forms for data entry. Once the templates have been created, no further HTML coding is necessary.

This technique is discussed in *Database-Driven Web Sites*. While it relies on databases to store and retrieve the Web page information, it is an application server that actually constructs the pages.

How Else to Do It

You can create those hundreds—or thousands—of Web pages manually. On an incremental basis, it is usually easier to create another Web page (to add to the hundreds that you already have) rather than to restructure your site to use dynamic pages, a database, and an application server. If you find yourself managing hundreds or thousands of Web pages, you might want to think about whether or not you are in this situation where the Web site could be better supported by using automated tools.

Another way in which large Web sites are maintained is to manually produce and update templates. Here, too, you may want to think about whether this is what has evolved in your organization. The symptoms of such a process are clear:

- You provide a template (or several) for the various types of pages on your site.

- You distribute the templates to users asking them to update them with their specific information and return them to you.

- Alternatively, you may have programs (such as Perl scripts) that merge user inputs to templates.

If you find yourself in these situations, you should realize that as your site grows the support effort will grow with it—often faster than the site.

Web-Integrated System Development

If you have the opportunity to design a system from scratch today, a Web-based interface is likely to be an integral part of that system. In fact, you may have a hard time convincing management to allow you to use any other type of interface (at least for a networked system—standalone systems often work best with other interfaces).

The Problem

Starting from scratch is a challenge and an opportunity. The first question is where to start in designing your system. You need an architecture that will work, can be delivered on time, and can be maintained throughout the years. No one starts out to write a legacy system, but all successful systems become legacy systems with the passage of time.

The Challenge

Building a Web-integrated system today requires that the designers and implementers understand the purpose of the system (the business logic), system design, interface design, and the current technologies in databases and the Web. Such skills are in high demand, and they do not always come packaged in any given individual. Moreover, the people who are interested in interface design (that is, working with people) are often not particularly interest in database design (that is, working with computers). Keeping abreast of all of these fields is more than a full-time job; it leaves little time for actually doing the work.

Where Application Servers Fit In

The architecture that revolves around application servers provides a simple way of structuring such system development projects. Because the interfaces to the application server are clearly defined (HTML on the interface side and SQL on the database side), people can work on subprojects with a minimum of coordination effort.

How Else to Do It

You can devise an alternative architecture to implement a Web-integrated system. It seems foolhardy to do so, but there are organizations that are experimenting with other architectures. Often in such cases you will find that the project in question turns out not to be a from-scratch new project: it actually is a modification to a legacy system, and that legacy architecture is what requires implementation of an idiosyncratic structure.

Another approach to the architecture of a Web-integrated system is to use a technology such as XML throughout the system. In a sense, this spreads the functionality of the application server through all of the system's components. Although tools such as XML can be very effective, such an architecture requires that all participants in the project understand the new technology. The use of application servers helps to compartmentalize new and old technologies.

| Personal Computer System Deployment | With the advent of personal computer networks in the late 1980s and 1990s, operations that theretofore might have been confined to mainframe networks were implemented on desktops. These networks of personal computers have grown in size, and the systems deployed on such networks are many and varied. |

Personal Computer System Deployment

With the advent of personal computer networks in the late 1980s and 1990s, operations that theretofore might have been confined to mainframe networks were implemented on desktops. These networks of personal computers have grown in size, and the systems deployed on such networks are many and varied.

The Problem

The problem in deploying personal computer-based systems is that they often do not scale well. The mainstream personal computer operating systems of the late 1990s (Windows 95/98 and Macintosh) have problems when they are pushed to support hundreds or thousands of network nodes. Newer systems (Windows NT, Mac OS X, and the various flavors of Unix) are more robust and can support the heavy demands of major distributed systems.

The Challenge

Unfortunately, not only are users familiar with desktop-based systems, but also many computer professionals are familiar with them and they may have most of their experience on unnetworked desktop computers (or at best on very small networks). The bread-and-butter of the mainframe systems programmer—complex test scenarios and multiple environments, intricate security mechanisms, and sophisticated load-balancing—are often news to desktop programmers.

In fact, many of the techniques developed in the 1960s and 1970s for time-sharing mainframe systems are being reinvented in the desktop environment. These issues are complex, but many of them lend themselves quite well to automation. Just as shoemakers' children are reputed to go barefoot, so programmers often are the last to benefit from automation and technology.

*Where
Application
Servers Fit In*

Application servers can be viewed as encapsulating several decades of experience on issues such as security and performance monitoring. Programmers need not reinvent mechanisms for preventing deadlock when two people try to access the same resource: instead, they can set parameters in the application server so that it will use a predefined strategy to prevent or eliminate such problems.

In some ways, application servers are programs whose users are system administrators (rather than end-users). Not only do they allow system administrators and programmers to avoid reinventing various wheels, but their collection of tools often suggest new problems—and solutions—to the administrators and programmers.

How Else to Do It

The alternative to application servers often is to extend and enhance existing desktop computer-based systems. The pitfalls of legacy systems apply here. Furthermore, it is common to see a project of such enhancement hit obstacle after obstacle as inexperienced staff tries to learn the intricacies of transaction processing and as desktop-based software is replaced with more and more powerful versions.

E-Commerce

By now it is routine to see estimates of large growth for e-commerce on the Web. It is equally common to see those estimates exceeded by realtiy. E-commerce is available to organizations large and small, and the fear of many large companies is that their smaller competitors will beat them to the punch. The price of entry to the electronic marketplace can be relatively low, and the stampede is on.

The Problem

E-commerce is a mission-critical system that can be similar to legacy systems in its importance to an organization. However, it is usually not only mission-critical but new in all aspects—hardware and software architectures as well as policy issues. And it all has to be done quickly.

The Challenge

E-commerce is new not only on the computer side but also on the business side. It is highly unlikely that today's e-commerce solutions will be those of tomorrow. The paradigms of shopping carts and online stores are firmly established, but they do not work well for all products. (Along with other organizations, *The New York Times* sells electronic copies of past articles for a few dollars. The shopping cart metaphor is nowhere to be found on that site.)

The late 1990s rise of online auctions for everything from yard-sale items to houses suggests to some people that the basic notions of commerce may change substantially in that direction—that is, to a negotiated price for items large and small.

An e-commerce implementation must be flexible so that as needs change it can move with the times. For many organizations, the e-commerce solution becomes the corporate face on the Internet, and it therefore acquires responsibilities that go far beyond selling goods.

Where Application Servers Fit In

Application servers often are at the heart of e-commerce solutions. Some are configured specifically for e-commerce. You can plug such an application server into your computing environment and let it interact with your database of inventory items and with the HTML pages that your designers create for a twenty-first century version of Macy's display windows.

In fact, the creation of e-commerce specific application server packages represents a significant opportunity in today's market. It suggests that many business-specific application server-based products may soon be on the market.

How Else to Do It

Many organizations have implemented e-commerce solutions as part of existing systems. However, the stringent demands of such solutions often lead to the use of third-party turn-key systems—which often are based on application servers.

Performance Management	The final paradigmatic use of application servers is to manage the performance of large systems with Web interfaces. While you may connect a single personal computer to the Internet in order to provide your site's information to the world, large installations require multiple servers and sophisticated load balancing.
The Problem	Performance management of large Web-based systems is a fine—and evolving—art. The public nature of such systems means that their operation reflects on the sponsoring organization; furthermore, the potential for extreme peaks and valleys of use makes it necssary to use the most sophisticated modeling and management tools to provide the best possibe service without devoting all of an organization's resources to network and computer management.
The Challenge	Web-integrated systems have a number of potential performance bottlenecks. On the database side, the tuning of a database for optimal performance is a complicated issue. On the interface (Web) side, tuning of the Web servers is equally complicated.
Where Application Servers Fit In	As noted previously, this type of problem is amenable to automated management. Application servers are on the market that contain sophisticated algorithms for performance management. In addition to providing performance management tools, some application servers are specifically geared to the problems of combining multiple databases and Web servers. They can be used to test high volume scenarios.
How Else to Do It	Vendors of databases and Web servers provide a variety of tools to tune and modify the performance of their products. Unfortunately, tuning each one separately does not always result in an optimal solution.

How Application Servers Work

Figure 2-1 shows an overview of the architecture of systems that use application servers. (This is a subset of the diagrams shown in Chapter 1; it focuses on the application server, eliminating the network.)

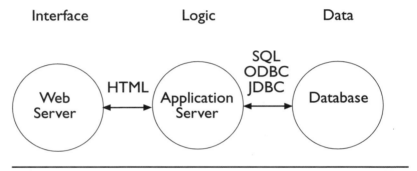

FIGURE 2-1. Application Server Architecture

As noted previously, application servers support Web servers by providing ad hoc HTML pages that often include data from databases. The Web server communicates with users (clients) using the standard HTTP Internet protocol, and it transmits HTML pages to those users (clients). The application server normally is unaware of HTTP; it simply serves up an HTML page on request. Both the Web server and application server use HTML for their common communication.

The application server communicates with databases using standard mechanisms such as SQL, ODBC, or JDBC. (See "Databases and Application Servers" starting on page 55 for more information.) This architecture allows data from the database to be transformed into HTML without writing any HTML code in the database. Likewise, the Web server can access database data without any SQL or ODBC code.

The use of standards in application servers is critical in constructing these systems: particularly in the case of legacy systems and databases, products from many vendors often need to coexist. Standards and open architectures make this possible.

In addition to standards and open systems, many proprietary protocols are used in the world of application servers. You will find servers that support many vendor-specific formats, and the benefits of this architecture accrue in those cases as well.

Many people like to note that this architecture separate the interface from the application logic and that both of those are separated from the data. This technique (known as **factoring**) allows for very efficient system development. However, it is important to note that these separations are not total. The design of the data in a database directly impacts both the logic and the interface (if the database does not store the date of a user's last visit to the site, the interface can't display, "Welcome back, Elvira").

There is more to this architecture than is shown in Figure 2-1. Figure 2-2 shows additional elements that are used by Web servers, application servers, and databases.

Note that each of the primary factors of the architecture (Web servers, application servers, and databases) can communicate with other elements (which are shown at the bottom of the figure). Communication with these other elements is generally not based on open standards; rather, it is defined by the specific product that is used. These additional elements may be provided by the vendors of the products involved, or they may be written by third parties or by end-users (or their technology staffs). More details on this part of the architecture are provided in Chapter 4, "Sub-Programs and Application Servers" starting on page 85.

As you can see from Figure 2-2, the application server is the center of this architecture: it provides standards-based interfaces to Web servers and to databases as well as a variety of interfaces to other elements (such as templates and software components) that enable it to do the necessary processing to carry out its tasks.

Note that the centrality of application servers in this diagram does not always coincide with promotional and marketing materials from vendors. Database vendors often provide application servers and even Web servers as part of their products; to no one's great surprise, in their diagrams the database is central.

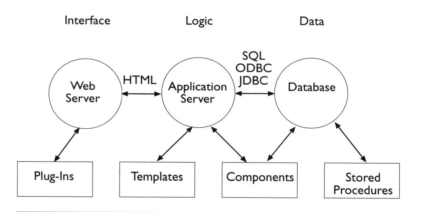

FIGURE 2-2. Detailed Application Server Architecture

An additional point of interest is that templates and components can be used both by Web and application servers (in the case of templates) and by application servers and databases (in the case of components). The boundaries between these conceptual components are not always so clear in the real world.

Types of Application Servers

While the architecture of application servers is fairly constant across many vendors' products, the terminology and specific design of each product is different. If you study white papers and promotional diagrams, you will almost always be able to find this architecture at the core of each one.

There are four types of application servers that you will find on the marketplace. The difference among them is primarily which parts of the architecture they encompass. Some bundle all three factors into a single entity, others integrate the application server into either the Web server or a database, and still others are a standalone architecture.

Operating Systems

The classic example of a complete bundle is Microsoft's approach to application servers. As the following statement shows, Microsoft's position is that its Windows NT Server operating system is an application server:

> Microsoft's application server technologies are a group of software services, which have been licensed for years with Windows NT Server, that support the creation of robust, scalable server applications accessible from browser and nonbrowser clients. Microsoft's application server technologies include common features such as support for building Web-based applications, support for transactions, a unifying component model, database connection pooling and load balancing. The integrated technologies composing the Microsoft application server include Microsoft Transaction Server, Active Server Pages, Internet Information Server, Microsoft Message Queue Services, and Component Object Model. [1]

1. "Compaq, CSC, ISVs and Key Customers Highlight Growing Momentum For Microsoft's Application Server Technologies" Feb 24 1999, http://www.microsoft.com/presspass/press/1999/feb99/serverpr.htm

The functions of an application server are distributed to a variety of operating system technologies that can be used together or (in some cases) separately. The database that is used can be Microsoft's SQL Server or any other database that is supported by ODBC.

Integrated

You will also find application servers that are integrated into Web servers or databases. FileMaker Pro, for example, bundles both a Web server and an application server into FileMaker Web Companion—which is a part of the FileMaker Pro package.

An integrated application server is part of a database or a Web server product. Unlike an architecture where the application server functions are distributed throughout the operating system and available for use by anyone who needs them, an integrated architecture may be a black box of functionality: you use all of it or none of it, and customization may be difficult.

Plug-In

Plug-in application servers are similar to integrated application servers in their design; however, rather than being part of another product (such as a database), they are shipped as separate components that you can plug into a Web server. Allaire Corporation's Cold Fusion is one such application server.

Standalone

Standalone application servers correspond exactly to the architecture shown in the figures of this chapter. You can place product names on the application server, Web server, and database. The boundaries of each factor of the architecture are those shown here.

Standalone application servers let you build your own system, mixing and matching Web servers and databases as you see fit. This can provide more flexibility (particularly if you are implementing a system in an environment where the Web server and/or database already exist). On the other hand, the long-standing tradeoff between the flexibility of a mix-and-match architecture and the apparent simplicity of a single-vendor solution remains a serious consideration.

| The Application Server Marketplace | The application server marketplace is in as much flux (if not more) than any aspect of Internet technology. This means that products are entering the marketplace at a rapid pace and then often leaving it—through failure or merger—at a similarly stunning pace. |

Every major vendor has an offering in the application server area (although some prefer to use another name for their technology). Smaller companies and start-ups have a secure place in the world of application servers—either directly or through their absorption into the major vendors' products.

It is useful to remember that in many ways application servers are similar to some of the mainframe products that have been used for years to monitor performance and to carry out very specialized tasks in the information technology areas of large organizations. This marketplace has long been characterized by small, highly specialized companies.

Furthermore, although some people might consider this heresy, the architecture that is centered on application servers is quite familiar to grizzled veterans of the information technology world. The notion of software that mediates between a database and a user interface system is familiar to programmers who used IBM's IMS in the 1970s and 1980s. Comparable products from other mainframe vendors (such as Burroughs) were used quite successfully in many applications. Some of those applications remain in use today.

What is different now is the degree of standardization of the interfaces. SQL and its associated technologies is the method for communicating with databases. HTTP and HTML are the methods for communicating with users; Internet browsers are the software for interacting with those users. Other technologies and proprietary standards may also be present, but these are the core technologies. The architecture, however, is several decades old. It works.

Application Servers and Middleware

If you look at architectural diagrams, you may see middleware occupying the spot that application servers do in the diagrams in this book. While there is a great deal of overlap, an argument can be made for making a distinction as follows.

Application servers mediate specifically between databases and Web servers. Middleware products and technologies mediate (form the middle) between system components that may be databases and Web servers—or other components. Furthermore, middleware technologies (being more general) may be applied to application servers.

Summary

This chapter has provided an overview of application servers and how they can be used. You have seen the types of jobs that they can do—and what other solutions can be applied to those problems.

The basic architecture of which application servers are a part has been reviewed—the triumvirate of Web servers, application servers, and databases, all linked by standard protocols and languages such as HTTP, HTML, and SQL.

Finally, the various types of application servers that are on the market today have been described. You will find application servers that are not identifiable as separate products but whose functionalities are scattered throughout an operating system. You will also find application servers that are part of databases or Web servers, and you will find standalone application servers that you can mix and match with various databases, Web servers, and operating systems.

The next chapter hones in on databases—a critical part of this architecture. The modern database that is part of an application server-based system may be a far cry from what you think of when you think of databases.

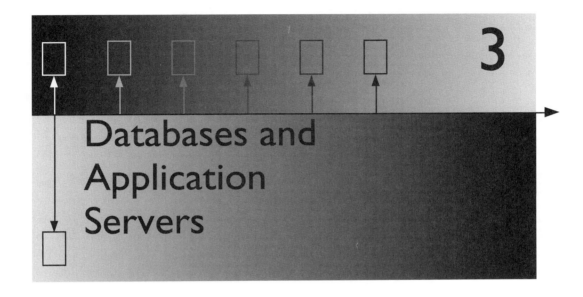

Databases and Application Servers

Databases are a critical companion to application servers. In fact, application servers are often defined as software that mediates between Web servers and databases.

You may be approaching application servers from the database side: in that case, the terminology is probably second-nature to you. You may also be approaching application servers from the Web server side: in that case, the terminology may be new.

The sections of this chapter deal with:

- *The state of the art of databases today,*

- *The relational model, and*

- *SQL.*

Databases: The State of the Art

Everyone knows what a database is, but it turns out that the terminology that "everyone knows" is not always clear. It is important to know how to talk about databases so as to avoid confusion. And once you have cleared the air, it is important to understand the types of databases that are in use today. Then, you may have to learn some new terms—such as data warehousing and data mining—to keep up with technology.

It is easy to forget that there are many forks in the technology road, and that some paths not taken have been taken over by underbrush. Since application servers often are implemented in a world of legacy systems, you may find yourself dealing with database technology that not only is old but is also from a technological world that no longer exists.

Here is a brief overview of the database world today.

Terminology

The word "database" is one of those terms that is frequently and ambiguously used—even by an individual. It can refer to a specific project (as in the subscriber database), a physical collection of data (stored in one or more files), and to a product that makes all of this possible (Oracle, DB2, FileMaker Pro, and others). Although the context usually makes the sense clear, this is the terminology that is used throughout this book:

- **Database projects** are projects implemented using database technology. They are implemented by programmers, consultants, or end-users. In mainframe environments, these are often called applications— payroll applications, accounting applications, and so forth. In the world of personal computers, applications of this sort are often called solutions. In both worlds they can also be called systems.

- **Databases** are the physical and logical collections of data that are stored on computers and made accessible through software. One or more databases are used to implement each database project. A database may be used in more than one database project. (A customer database, for example, may be part of a billing database project and/or a marketing support project.)

- **Database Management Systems (DBMSs)** are the software products that make this all possible. They are developed by companies such as Oracle, Microsoft, and IBM.

DBMSs in Use Today

The range of database management systems today is broad, ranging from mainframe-based products that require information technology staff to support them all the way to shrink-wrapped products for desktop computers. An additional segment of the market consists of embedded database products that are part of everything from handheld devices to personal accounting software on personal computers and to Web site support systems.

This last segment is increasingly important: as the software industry for personal computers has changed and consolidated over the years, many companies have found themselves developing and supporting products that were initially designed by other companies. Idiosyncratic data storage systems have proven in many cases to be costly maintenance headaches.

Databases Are Getting Bigger

Databases are growing in size at an enormous rate. In the case of databases that track transactions, this is because once they have been set up and automated data collection mechanisms put in place, they tend to keep growing.

In the past, it was often necessary to archive old data; keeping it around just wasted disk space and often degraded the performance of the DBMS. Today, that is not necessarily the case.

Storage Is Getting Cheaper   The cost of computer storage is dropping (as are all computer costs). This cost is reflected in two ways:

1. You can buy a hard disk today for less than it cost a year ago.

2. You can buy much more disk today for the same price that you paid a year ago.

In fact, the prices of disk storage have not dropped as much as you might expect. Rather, the second point comes into play: the computer that you buy today has a hard disk measured in gigabytes (billions of bytes); the computer you bought a year or two ago had a hard disk measured in megabytes (millions of bytes).

The consequence of the drop in price of computer storage is often much more available space to the average user (or corporation). Old timers (from a few years ago) can remember spending hours archiving and unarchiving files so that they could move from one project to another. Today, many people simply do not run out of disk space on their personal computers.

Furthermore, technologies such as **RAID**—redundant arrays of inexpensive disks—provide performance and reliability that were unheard-of only a few years ago. A decade ago, the concept of disk mirroring—whether duplicate copies of data are stored on duplicate disks—was reserved for transaction processing systems at stock exchanges and the like. Today, it is an option for the desktop user.

Computers Are Getting More Powerful   Of course, the ability to store boundless amounts of data is meaningless if it takes forever to access that data. Advances in computer hardware technology have made data access speedier than ever and have minimized the problems of very large databases.

Not only are processors faster than ever, but more and more computers and their operating systems are supporting **symmetric multiprocessing (SMP)** in which several processor chips divide up the work while sharing other resources (such as memory and disk). The apparent barriers to performance that exist at the single chip level are easily broken when you put several chips together.

Databases Are Getting Smaller

At the same time that corporate databases are getting bigger, databases that are accessible from hand-held devices (and that are even fully implemented on hand-held devices) are gaining favor. Often these databases are synchronized with larger databases—as when a single meter reader's hand-held device has its data merged into a town's water meter database.

Data Is More Diverse Than Ever

Data is no longer numeric and alphanumeric data. Data now includes graphics, video, and sound. Such data is usually relatively large when compared to numeric data. Furthermore, the tools that are used to manipulate graphic, video, and sound data when it is retrieved often include searching mechanisms. This has the effect of sometimes placing database-like data within a database.

Data Needs to Be More Accessible

Originally, databases were positioned largely as a tool to help programmers implement projects. ("You'll never have to write input/output routines again.") Sharing data between and among projects through databases gradually became a goal that was recognized but not always achieved. In part, this was because each project was designed separately. When an organization-wide data strategy was formulated, it often was obsolete by the time it was completed. By the late 1980s, it was routine to hear of companies with scores (literally) of incompatible systems and databases; redundant and inconsistent data was the norm.

At one bank, a task force was established to find out exactly how many customer databases existed. The members of the task force were flabbergasted to discover that only 13 separate name-and-address databases existed. Most guesses would have placed that number between 20 and 50.

Databases Are Merging and Communicating

Techniques have been emerging over the last decade that allow databases to share and combine their data. This has been accomplished in many ways, but the end result is that data in one vendor's database (such as IBM's DB2) can be used in conjunction with data in another vendor's database (such as Microsoft's SQL Server)—even if the two databases are on two different types of computers (such as an IBM mainframe and a Sun workstation).

Organizations have often allowed their data to be held hostage by vendors of hardware and software. Today, it is increasingly the case that organizations are reclaiming their data, and demanding that it be accessible to them as they see fit—regardless of the hardware and software that they have used to collect and store the data.

Data Warehousing

One way in which this is happening is with the advent of **data warehousing**—hardware, software, and associated technologies that help organizations combine their various data stores into a single enterprise-wide resource. Data warehouses are typically copies (as in duplicates) of operational or transaction data. (To use an ancient metaphor, a data warehouse is like the carbon copies of sales slips.)

Data in a data warehouse gets there through periodic updates from the live databases that support operations and transactions. These periodic updates (which often take place in off hours) are the only way in which data warehouse data is modified. As a result, most users of data warehouses perceive them as read-only data sources.

Data warehouses typically contain detailed data—information down to the invoice level, for example. Summary data has traditionally been used to track an organization's operations; however, by having access to the detailed data, trends that are hidden in averages and other summaries can be spotted.

Data warehouses are often used in **online analytical processing (OLAP)**. These are databases and specialized software that facilitate ad hoc queries by users. Data can come from a variety of sources; in the data warehouse the data is accessible as if its format and structure were specified from an organization's point of view. In other words, the possibly idiosyncratic data structures that may support specific applications are usually not carried over into the data warehouse—although the data itself is stored there. This is important not only because the data warehouse is primarily geared for use by end users who are doing analysis but also because it is designed without the regard for update performance that transaction systems require.

Data Mining   The way in which this is done is with data mining: technologies that allow users to analyze the raw data in a data warehouse quickly and efficiently in an online environment. Often the data warehouse data is combined with outside data (particularly demographic data in the case of marketing applications). The structure of the data allows manipulation of data from a variety of databases as if it contained similar underlying data—which it often does.

The impact of data mining and data warehousing on some organizations cannot be over-emphasized. The immediate access to raw data is something that statisticians often only dream of. In traditional statistical analyses, the data is frequently quite simple, reflecting averages of a variety of individual observations; the statistical analyses are often quite complex. With these tools, the data is quite complex—in many cases, absolutely no summarization has taken place. As a result, the statistical analyses are often quite simple: there is no need to extrapolate.

The Great Database Secrets

Finally, it is important to note that databases are among the most mature of computer software products. This means that while they may not be quite so flashy as the latest Internet technologies, they are often among the most reliable and high-quality products around. The kinks of the 1960s, 1970s, 1980s, and 1990s have been worked out. Furthermore, databases have seen it all—from the first attempts at time-sharing on mainframes to the latest experiments with fragmented databases that are implemented on wireless hand-held devices.

Reliability, synchronization, concurrency, transaction processing, roll-backs, documentation, and security: these have all been topics of conversation (as well as experiment and implementation) for decades. Database software is typically tried and true.

In addition, the major database products have quite comparable features and prices. It is no surprise that each major database vendor now has an application server product. Their biggest clients tend not to switch databases, but each client wants all of the current technologies made available.

Databases on the Desktop

Personal-computer-based database products include such stalwarts as the FoxBase/dBase products, FileMaker Pro, Microsoft Access, and a variety of other products. The FoxBase/dBase products are among the oldest—and in fact the products are no longer widely sold. However, databases using these products are still in widespread use.

FileMaker Pro remains a major player on the desktop market; Microsoft Access is a product in transition as Microsoft encourages users to consider moving to SQL Server.

What This Means for Application Servers	Application servers provide links between the interfaces of Web servers and the data in databases. Those databases may be "live"—the transaction-oriented databases that are updated constantly as events happen, or they may be the static data warehouses that contain copies of completed transactions.
Making the Impossible Happen	The database that served primarily as a programmer's tool to simplify reading and writing data is being replaced by the database that is a corporate asset, the data of which is needed not only for transaction but also for analysis. From the point of view of programmers and an information technology staff, the biggest corporate goal may be standardizing platforms and database systems; but from the point of view of management, the primary goal is likely to be to implement the kind of open functionality that was described and illustrated in the figures of Chapter 2.
	This means that corporate management may well draw diagrams from one database to another and from one computer environment to another without regard for whether or not those products and platforms actually are capable of communicating with one another. Management's argument is that that isn't their problem—and besides, they need it to happen. Application servers are ideally suited for making this happen.
Regularizing the Enterprise Information Environment	More and more organizations are viewing their information resources in some variety of the architecture discussed here. Public databases (at least within the organization) are accessible to a variety of queries and updates—either directly or through their data warehouse copies. Acceptance of this architecture is different from the choice of specific hardware or software products: it is an architecture that has evolved over several decades, and little risk is involved.
	If your organization uses other architectures (or none—as in an ad hoc environment that has just grown like Topsy), it may be time to move toward this type of architecture. That move

may be little more than renaming your modules and systems, recognizing that this architecture is really not particularly revolutionary. In some cases, it means planning for the elimination of non-database systems; usually these are legacy systems that have brought with them ancient databases (or custom-written input/output routines).

| What Ever Happened to... | As with any technology, databases have had some false starts and blind alleys. At the time, it is not always clear where the mainstream will be: you may have legacy systems that incorporate some of these no-longer current technologies. |

Database Machines

In the late 1980s, special-purpose database computers were developed, and some actually came onto the market. Their hardware and operating systems were optimized for the sorts of operations that databases need to do (heavy input/output, manipulation of indices, and so forth).

With the advent of ever more powerful computers, the special-purchase technology has seemed less critical. Today, database machines are often standard computers that are dedicated to that purpose through management rather than hardware configuration.

Data Dictionaries and Data Models

In the mid-1980s, corporate data dictionaries and data models were the rage. The idea was to develop an enterprise-wide data management schema that would encompass all of an organization's operations. In its extreme manifestation, this led to writing (or rewriting) all of an organization's software. In less extreme manifestations, it led to a roadmap to which new systems were expected to adhere.

Unfortunately, it was often the case that in the time it took to come up with an organization's data dictionary and data model, the organization had changed—through merger or acquisition, general business developments, or other normal events. This Soviet-style approach to data management has been responsible for many over-budget projects and much misunderstanding.

If you compare this central-planning approach to the philosophy behind today's data warehousing approach, you will note that data warehousing allows an organization's systems to be developed and operate in the ways that are best to them. The data is then copied and manipulated as necessary as it is stored in the data warehouse. This tries to combine the best of centralization and local control.

Non-Relational Models

Almost all databases in use today are relational. Other databases exist (and have existed). Three of the most important non-relational databases are inverted lists, hierarchic databases, and network databases.

Inverted list databases are an outgrowth of flat files. The contents of fields within the flat files are copied to a separate file; as a result, you can read all of the values for a given field from the inverted file. You can locate the value(s) in which you are interested and then read those records. Index-Sequential Access Method (ISAM) files are examples of inverted list databases.

Inverted lists are often used for indexing text information; today, such inverted lists are used by search engines to index Web pages. In this case, there are no explicit fields—just a long string of text. The non-noise words (words other than "and," "whereas," and so forth) are extracted from the text; then a record for each word is created or updated with the URL on which the word was located. In this way, a record for the word "database" can be built that contains URLs for Web pages containing that word. Likewise, a record for "invert" can be built. (Words are "stemmed"—so "inverted" is stored under "invert".) To find all URLs for inverted list databases, the records for invert, list, and database are compared, and the URLs common to all three are presented.

Hierarchic databases are somewhat more structured than inverted list databases. Here, data is grouped logically. You may have a data element called Department; within that you may have Manager. Within Manager you may have Phone Number. IBM's IMS is an example of a hierarchic database.

The problem with hierarchic databases is that they quickly become complex and redundant. An individual who is a manager of a department can also be an employee of another manager—databases are much less flexible than the real world.

Network databases attempt to deal with the complexity of hierarchic databases by allowing nodes to be related to one another in many ways. This handles the situation well, but its complexity quickly exceeds the grasp of most people. An example of a network databases is Cullinane Corporation's IDMS.

It is noteworthy that hierarchic and network databases quickly become so complex that many organizations impose arbitrary limits on the number of levels that one can employ. Particularly with the needs to share data, it is important that the data be organized in logical ways and that it can be used by a variety of people using a variety of tools.

The Relational Model

The relational model of database design is very simple. Data is placed in tables—two-dimensional matrices that look like spreadsheets. Each column represents a type of data—address, ID number, age, and so forth. Each row represents one observation—one person, one inventory item, or one URL.

Relational databases allow you to join tables (or parts of tables) to construct very complex collections of data—collections of data just as complex as in any hierarchic or network database. What sets the relational model apart is that these complex data constructions are dynamic—created as needed. The data itself is stored in the simple two-dimensional tables.

Not only is data stored in tables, but the results of database operations in a relational database are themselves tables. These new tables may be collections of data from one or more tables or they may be subsets of data from one or more tables; still, at every step of the way, you are dealing with tables.

These intermediate tables may be transient, as opposed to the "real" tables that are stored on disk. From your point of view as a programmer or end-user, it does not matter if the table is real or transient.

Beyond this basic tenet—that everything is a table—there are a few other things that you need to know about relational databases. The following section introduces you to the terminology and to the critical issue of normalization.

Terminology

The terms used in the relational model are simple English words. The most basic ones come in pairs: one element of the pair is a common word (with ambiguous meanings); the other is more precise and is based on mathematical set theory.

As noted previously, all data in relational databases is stored in **tables**. A table is also called a **relation**.

Note that the physical storage is up to the database management system. A relational database presents data to the user as if it were in tables, whether or not that is the case.

Each **row** of the table contains the data for one observation (one individual, one inventory item, etc.). A row is also called a **tuple**.

Each **column** of the table contains the data for one **field** or **attribute**. A column can represent the age, ID number, color, or address of the row in the table—people, inventory items, Web sites, etc.

A **primary key** is a field that contains a unique value for each row in the table. An ID number can be a primary key. Names, addresses, colors, and similar attributes are not necessarily unique and are generally not used as primary keys. Relational databases allow you to enforce uniqueness of primary keys so that people cannot add duplicate names or other values to primary keys.

A **domain** is the universe of legal value for an attribute (or field or column). As with primary keys, database software often lets you enforce this so that you do not wind up with a value for color of "dog." Frequently you need to write special add-on software to enforce these rules.

The **cardinality** of a table is the number of rows it contains, and the **degree** of a table is the number of columns it contains.

When data is moved into a data warehouse, it is frequently restructured and reorganized so that logically related data for the warehouse is collected even though in reality such data may come from a variety of databases. Data warehouses use the term **dimension** to refer to such a logical structure. Dimensions can be concepts such as time or location; they collect database fields such as month, day, and year or city, state or province, and country. In other cases, the dimension of a multi-dimensional database is in fact a single two-dimensional database.

Normalization

A great deal of the power of relational databases comes from the simplicity of the core concept—the table—and the power of the ad hoc combinations and extractions that can be performed. In order to keep the basic tables simple and to facilitate operations on them, relational database tables are normalized. **Normalization** means that the data has a simpler structure than if it is unnormalized. ("Simple" is used in its strict mathematical sense. The structure may be quite complex, but no less complex structure can be found.)

Normalization derives from logic, set theory, and mathematics. It seems very cut and dried and quite elegant. Unfortunately, in the real world, normalization is frequently more of an art than a science.

In the first place, it requires an understanding of the meaning of the data in the database that goes far beyond writing down the names of the fields. In a very simple case, it is important to know whether or not color can be a unique key. In the case of children's blocks, it probably is not a unique identifier of a block; however, in a book of paint samples, color is a unique key.

Furthermore, in the case of a shared database, the meaning of the data can change subtly from one user to another. If you think that this is impossible, consider that wars have been fought over the meanings of words. Normalization matters because these are the rules that people use to organize their data. You may need to normalize your own data, and in such cases you need to know not only what the rules are but also what aspects of the data are relevant to the rules.

There are five normal forms; they are progressively more complex. The first normal form is a given for relational databases: if they do not adhere to it, they are not relational. The first three normal forms are normally employed on most relational databases. The fourth and fifth forms are used in some cases. (Not all relational database texts recognize fourth and fifth normal forms; they were proposed in the late 1970s, whereas the relational model and the first three normal forms date from 1970.)

First Normal Form: Eliminate Repeating Groups

This is the cardinal rule of relational databases. Consider a table that stores inventory information for a company that has several warehouses. A typical data record might look like the structure shown in Table 3-1.

Inventory Table

Part ID

Warehouse 1 Name

On Hand in Warehouse 1

On Order for Warehouse 1

Warehouse 2 Name

On Hand in Warehouse 2

On Order for Warehouse 2

Warehouse 3 Name

On Hand in Warehouse 3

On Order for Warehouse 3

TABLE 3-1. Inventory Table with Repeating Groups

There are three repeating groups in this structure. For each warehouse there is a field for its name, for the quantity on hand, and another for the quantity on order. This violates the first normal form, and causes at least three potential problems:

1. Each record contains the information for up to three warehouses. This works as long as no part is stored in more than three warehouses. If a part is stored in only one or two warehouses, space is wasted.

2. It is difficult to search efficiently. If you want to find the inventory in a certain warehouse, you have to read

each record and check if that warehouse is identified in any of the three fields.

3. Getting around these limitations brings out terrifying creativity in database designers and users. For a part that is stored in more than three warehouses, you can create duplicate records for that part (perhaps adding a –1 or –2 to the part number).

What Are Repeating Fields?   One type of work-around for some of the limitations of this database structure is shown in Table 3-2. Some people might think that this table structure no longer has repeating groups—after all, each field is identified with a unique warehouse.

Inventory Table

Part ID

On Hand in Valatie Warehouse

On Order for Valatie Warehouse

On Hand in Hudson Warehouse

On Order for Hudson Warehouse

On Hand in Ghent Warehouse

On Order for Ghent Warehouse

TABLE 3-2. Inventory Table with Implicit Repeating Groups

However, there are still problems:

1. It makes the warehouse structure part of the table. If the company closes one warehouse or opens another, all table records need to be modified.

2. It is still difficult to search. If you want to calculate the total inventory of parts in the Ghent Warehouse, you must read all records. Furthermore, if you want to find any warehouse that has a specific part, you also must search all records.

This points up a problem that occurs frequently in database design: what one person sees as repeating fields another person may see as unique identifiers. That is why database design requires judgment and discussion; automated design tools usually require some fiddling along the way.

A Normalized Table Structure   The correct structure for such a table is to use two related tables, as shown in Table 3-3.

Warehouse Table	**Inventory Table**
Warehouse ID	Warehouse ID
Warehouse Name	Part ID
	On Hand
	On Order

TABLE 3-3. Normalized Inventory Table

The Warehouse Table contains an identifier for the warehouse along with its name. In reality, it would contain a variety of other fields such as address, telephone number, and so forth. The Inventory Table contains information about a specific part in a specific warehouse. To find the name of the warehouse, you need to look in the Warehouse Table (using the Warehouse ID used in both tables).

There are only as many records in the Inventory Table as are needed: if a warehouse has no items in stock, it has a record in the Warehouse table, but no part records in the Inventory table. Similarly, for a part that is stored in scores of warehouses, there is no problem fitting that information into a record that assumes a maximum of 3 (or 10 or 100) warehouses.

At this point, you might wonder if there is a trade-off between the simplicity of the database structure and the reality of performance. After all, this structure requires multiple table access to obtain full inventory information (including warehouse names). The table structures shown previously allow all the information for a part to be stored in one record and retrieved with one disk access.

The answer is that storage space is getting cheaper and data access is getting faster. What is getting scarcer and more expensive is programmer time. Particularly with modern databases that use sophisticated caching algorithms to minimize disk access, the theoretical performance degradation due to multiple accesses required in a normalized database is not particularly noticeable.

Second Normal Form: Eliminate Redundant Data

If you are worried about performance, you might be tempted to slip the warehouse name into the Inventory Table along with the Warehouse ID. After all, it is just a few characters, and it will save an extra disk access when you are producing reports.

Don't do this: it violates the second normal form—eliminate repeating data. There is a very good reason for this rule. Simply put, redundant data poses a very high risk of being incorrect. If the warehouse name were placed in the Inventory table, then every part record would have the name of the warehouse to which it applied in that record. What would you do if the warehouse name changed? Change thousands of Inventory Table records? Using the meaningless warehouse ID to link the inventory and warehouse records, you can safely change the warehouse name (once—in the Warehouse Table), and rely on its appearing correctly everywhere else.

Long-time database designers are very fond of meaningless identifiers. As soon as you incorporate information into an identifier—such as its name—you start violating the second normal form (at least in spirit).

When Is Data Redundant?　　Just as with the first normal form, there are very legitimate issues to be raised about the specific data involved. Redundant data may be obvious—like the name of the warehouse, but it also can be more esoteric.

Consider the case of a table that contains invoice information. You might well have a related table that contains the name and price for each item number on the invoice. By placing the item number on the invoice, you can—on demand—retrieve the subsidiary information from the secondary table.

But what if this is a billing invoice? What if you need to store the price that was charged at the moment the sale was completed? (Your secondary table might well contain the current price.) In such a case, it is quite reasonable to store the price in the invoice table—although at first it will be redundant. Over time, as prices change, it will be clear that the data is not redundant. It will be inconsistent—as it should be. The invoice should reflect the price charged at the time of the sale, not the current price.

Conversely, a catalog table might be required to take the price from an item table so that there is no chance that there will be a discrepancy. Remember that database design requires that you understand the data and the uses to which it will be put.

What to Do with Redundant Data　　There are two basic approaches to dealing with redundant data. You can pull the redundant data out into a separate table, or you can make certain that the data is not truly redundant. As in the case of prices that may change over time, calling a field in the item table Current Item Price and a field in the invoice table Price

Billed makes it clear that you are not dealing with exactly the same data item.

You will find redundant data repeatedly as you look at existing databases; a perfectly normalized database created for one system may duplicate data in another database that was created by other people in another location in your organization. Stomping your feet and demanding that people change database structures that are working is not the best way of dealing with the issue. The only solution to this problem is to understand the data and what it is that you need to do with it. (This is a frequent challenge for data warehouses: they must constantly deal with factually inconsistent but logically equivalent data.)

Third Normal Form: Eliminate Fields Not Dependent on Key

The classic example of this issue is an address database that contains postal codes and town names. You can use such an address to look up the postal code for a given town and vice versa. However, the database only works in this way for the postal codes and towns that are represented in the addresses it contains.

The solution—once again—is to split the data into separate tables. In an extreme case, you store only the postal code or the town name in the database—a separate database provides a complete look-up of all town names and postal codes. Again, judgment comes into play: for small data items such as postal codes and town names, violating the third normal form often is not a terrible mistake. However, be aware that people may soon come to rely on your unnormalized table to look up postal codes and towns—and they may not find them.

SQL

Originally an acronym, SQL is now a name in and of itself. Its goal is that of manipulating something called SQL-data—that subset of relational data that it handles properly. (There are some types of relational data that cannot be manipulated by SQL, but they are not common in the types of applications discussed in this book.)

The most critical point to remember about SQL is that it is declarative rather than procedural. This section outlines the meaning and significance of that statement. It also provides you with a brief overview of SQL syntax. The syntax is not particularly complicated, and many resources are available both as books and as online references. This section give you a basic overview of the major points.

Procedural Versus Declarative Programming

The most important aspect of SQL is that it is declarative rather than procedural. Traditional programming (just like traditional manual procedures in offices, factories, and other environments) is primarily procedural. In such procedural cases, operations are described something like this:

- Get the first that is… (on the assembly line, in the incoming mail, etc.).

- Test it to determine what to do to it.

- Do whatever is necessary.

- Get the next (from the assembly line, in the incoming mail, etc.) and repeat until there are no more.

In declarative programming, there is a simpler structure:

- Get all that are (on the assembly line, in the incoming mail) and that require a specific thing to be done to them. (This is the first two points of the previous list.)

- Do what is neccessary to each of them.

The test in the procedural method (determine what to do to each item) is incorporated in the first step: you get everything that will need a certain operation performed on it. This makes for much simpler processing, since the internal tests on each item are no longer necessary.

Note that this type of programming that starts with "get all that are…" may turn out to get no records or to get a single record. In fact, you may logically know that only one record will satisfy the "get all that are…" request. Nevertheless, even when you are dealing with a single record, the structure of declarative program is the structure that is shown here.

Structured programming (which was developed during the 1970s) got rid of "spaghetti code"—computer code with goto statements that caused execution to jump around and made it hard for people to read programs. Declarative programming goes further and gets rid of conditional statements (since they are incorporated into the initial statement that gets everything with certain characteristics). The result is that the code that is written now is executed from start to finish—without jumps or conditions. Such code is easy to read and to test: there is only one execution sequence.

If you get into the spirit of declarative programming, you will find that some of your time-honored ideas about programming may change. In procedural programs, you often store a great deal of transient information about the data you are working on. You may have variables that indicate whether a report should be generated in summary or in detail; you may have flags that tell you if accounting should be done as of the first or last of the month; or you may have indicators that warn users about possible problems.

In declarative programming, this information is stored in database tables. In its purest incarnation, declarative programming consists of little besides SQL statements; furthermore,

SQL provides no variables to use. Thus, the database tables at any given moment reflect not only the data but all of the transient information about the data that might be needed for work at that time. Old-timers may hem and haw about the inefficiency of having to do disk accesses to get this additional information; but, as noted before, modern databases use caching to keep performance good.

This structure—in which the state of transactions and other operations is stored in the database rather than in a program's memory locations—is highly compatible with HTTP which is a stateless protocol. If you have attempted to implement any kind of Web-based system other than one that simply displays prepared HTML pages, you will know how difficult it is to keep such data easily available.

Basic SQL Syntax

SQL is used within programs written in other programming languages such as Cobol, C, C++, Visual Basic, or Java. You normally do not write a program in SQL alone.

Select

Whether you type your query in text or design it using a graphical user interface, you are usually creating SQL queries. (Even in those cases when you are not, the designers of the database often think in SQL terms and they map their query language to SQL either consciously or unconsciously.)

The most basic SQL statement is the Select statement; it operates on one or more tables and creates a result—a new table. Although the Select statement can be very complicated, its basis is quite simple:

```
Select column(s) FROM table(s)
<WHERE condition>
<GROUP BY condition
    <HAVING grouped characteristic>>
```

SubQueries   Since the result of a Select statement is a table, you can use a Select statement in the From clause of a Select statement, as in

```
Select Name, Age From
    (Select Name, Age, Address From Customers Where Age > 18)
```

(Although in this case the statement could be expressed in a single Select statement, many complex statements benefit from this multilayered construction of Select statements.)

Select *   Instead of specifying the columns to be retrieved, you can ask for all columns of a table to be selected by using an asterisk, as in

```
Select * from Customers
```

(This is the shortest Select statement that can be constructed— it returns all rows and columns from the table mentioned in the Select statement.)

Where Conditions   Where clauses can specify comparison values (such as Age > 18) as well as set operations such as IN. You can create a temporary table (using a Select statement, of course) and use that temporary table to test whether rows from your primary select statement will be used.

Group By/Having   The Group By clause lets you group the returned rows by some value (often a calculated value, such as a sum or average). When the Having clause is used as well, you can include only the rows from groups having certain characteristics (a sum greater than X, an average less than Y, etc.).

Examples of Select Statements   Here are some typical Select statements:

```
Select Names from Customers
```

This could select all customer names from a Customers table.

```
Select Names from Customers where Balance > 100.00
```

This could select all customers with balances greater than 100 from a Customers table.

```
Select Names from Customers where Balance > 100.00 ORDER BY Bal-
ance
```

This query is the same as the last except that the results will be sorted from smallest to largest balance.

Queries can operate against several tables at the same time; in such cases, column names need to be qualified with table names as in this query and the relationship between records in the two tables needs to be expressed. In this query, records are drawn from both the Customers and the Accounting tables; the tables are matched on a field called ID that exists in both tables:

```
SelectNames, Balances from Customers, Accounting Where Custom-
ers.ID=Accounting.ID.
```

It is the section Customers.ID=Accounting.ID that links the records from the two tables (assuming that a unique customer ID exists in both Customers and Accounting—and that it is the same ID for both files). Creating a table from two underlying tables using a common field is called a **join**.

Cursors

A cursor is associated with a table that is created as the result of some database operation (such as finding all records that are…). The cursor can be positioned on, after, or before any row in the table. When it is so positioned, the data for that row can be manipulated by the program, and the cursor is typically advanced to the next row.

The most significant database access occurs when the cursor is opened—that is, when its associated table is constructed via a query. Subsequent accesses (retrieving each row) typically involve much less database horsepower.

Insert   The SQL Insert command inserts a row of data into a table. The data must often adhere to certain edits (such as having a unique key, having numeric values for certain fields). You will often use an Insert command to add data to your database-driven Web sites, although the application server you use will often generate it for you automatically.

Commonly, the data that is inserted into the database is collected from a user using an HTML form.

Delete   The SQL Delete command deletes a row of data that is specified using the appropriate unique key. Again, edits may come into play to prevent you from deleting part of related records in several tables (referential integrity).

As with Insert, you often do not see this code—it is generated for you by your application server software.

Update   The SQL Update command modifies data in an existing row of a table. You can use variations of the Update command to perform mass updates (such as multiplying all values by a constant). The difference between Insert and Update is that Insert creates a new row and Update modifies an existing row.

Create   A variety of SQL Create statements let you create the objects of relational databases. These include tables as well as subsidiary structures such as views and indexes.

Views   Views can be considered temporary tables. The result of a select is always a table; such a table can be saved as a view. It does not actually exist as a table, but you can refer to the view as if it were a table. Each time you refer to the view, the Select statement that created it is effectively re-executed, along with its conditions and criteria.

Indexes   Database software uses whatever information it has at hand to fulfill your queries. It can create indexes to the data in the database—and you can create indexes yourself. This can be useful when you know how the data will be retrieved.

ODBC and
JDBC

In the early 1990s, Microsoft released its Open Database Connectivity (ODBC). Based on the SQL standard and work done by other organizations (including the X/Open Call-Level Interface and the SQL Access Group's SQL ComputerAided Engineering specification of 1992—SAG SQL CAE), ODBC is an application programming interface (API) that combines with a set of run-time libraries to allow dynamic access to various databases.

In your program, you write your SQL database calls using the ODBC standard. At runtime, the ODBC library connects to a specific database driver that converts the standard ODBC calls to Oracle calls, DB2, calls, SQL server calls—or even calls to non-databases such as Excel spreadsheets or flat files. Everything from field names to database names can be modified at runtime. This enables you to write to an abstract database that is concretized only at runtime.

Recently, a companion API called **Java Database Connectivity (JDBC)** has been developed to perform these same operations in the Java environment.

Summary

Almost all databases today are based on the relational model; they use SQL as their primary data manipulation language. Because of this standardization, it is possible to incorporate databases from a variety of vendors into standard architectural designs—such as those that use application servers.

Application servers are intimately connected to relational databases using SQL as well as to Web servers. All of this is made possible with a variety of technologies; most significant is the rise of component software. That is the topic of the next chapter.

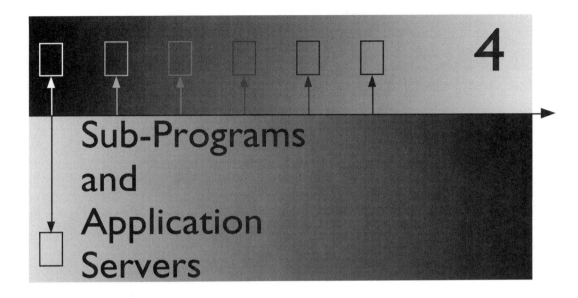

Sub-Programs and Application Servers

Sub-programs are present in many guises—scripts, applets, serv-lets, plug-ins, helper applications, and stored procedures. They interact with programs according to a variety of protocols and interfaces—CGI, ISAPI, NSAPI, HTTP, and HTML. This chapter explores those terms and the processes that use them.

Specifically, you will find out about

- *what sub-programs are,*
- *client-side programming,*
- *server-side programming,*

- *interface protocols and APIs, and*
- *basic protocols.*

What Are Sub-Programs?

The classical view of computer software is that of programs that process data; a sharp distinction is drawn between the programs themselves and their inputs and outputs. However, from the earliest days of modern computers this distinction has been arbitrary, misleading, and in many cases false. (Pioneers such as VonNeumann and Hopper all recognized that the distinction between the bits and bytes of data and the bits and bytes of instructions were human projections.)

Output from one program (a compiler) can actually be a program itself, and a program can be input to another program (such as an operating system). As soon as you recognize that programs have a great deal in common with data, you may want to exploit this fact. One common way of doing so is by creating small programs—sub-programs—that can be used in conjunction with traditional programs.

Client and Server Sub-Programs	Sub-programs can be used to augment any part of the application server architecture. Their terminology differs depending on the type of sub-program they are and where they are used. Figure 4-1 shows the terminology for sub-programs used on Web browsers (at the user's computer) and for Web servers (at the server or host computer).

Note that although only a Web server is shown, the same terminology that applies to Web servers also can apply to application servers and to some databases. Sub-programs can be stand-alone programs or they can be incorporated into the browser and Web server at run-time; both architectures are suggested by the figure. Furthermore, note that in some cases the sub-programs are capable of communicating with other devices and programs—as the arrow at the right of the figure suggests.

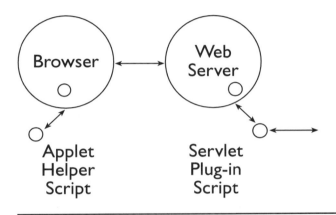

FIGURE 4-1. Sub-Programs for Browsers and Servers

Types of Sub-Programs

Sub-programs fall into three basic categories:

1. Helper applications and plug-ins,

2. Applets and servlets, and

3. Scripts.

No matter what category of subprogram you are dealing with, it is important to know the following:

- What language is it written in?

- Where does it run?

- How is it executed?

Applets and Servlets	Applets and servlets are frequently written in a language such as Java and Visual Basic; they are executed by the browser or server using a virtual machine (which often is a process that runs elsewhere on the computer). Using a language such as Java, these sub-programs can be written once and then compiled to an intermediate set of instructions called **byte code**; the byte code is platform-independent, and it is executed by the virtual machine.

They may be executed for a variety of reasons; typically it is because an event has occurred to which they are tied. (Such events can be user interface events—mouse movements on a Web page—or operational events—a user log on, for example.) |
| **Helper Applications and Plug-Ins** | Helper applications and plug-ins are normally written in a programming language such as C++ or C. As such they need to be written and compiled for each platform on which they are used. They are distributed in the form of object code, and they are executed as needed by the browser or server.

They may run as a separate process or as a procedure called by the browser or server. In the latter case, they use the browser or server's memory partition. They are frequently executed in order to handle a data type that the browser or server does not natively support.

Helper applications are familiar to Web browser users: they are the applications that process types of data or protocols that the browser does not deal with itself. When you download a video clip, a formatted document, or a compressed file, you typically need to use a helper application to expand and display the data correctly. |
| *File Helpers* | When such data is detected, the browser launches the appropriate helper application; it may run as a plug-in to the brows- |

er or as a stand-alone application. If it runs as a plug-in, the helper application processes the data and returns it to the browser for display within the page. (That is how video is often displayed.) If it runs as a stand-alone application, the data is displayed within the helper application's own window.

Mapping Files to Helpers   The connection between a specific helper application and a file type is accomplished using file suffixes and Multipurpose Internet Mail Extension (MIME) types. (The problem of connecting a specific type of data to a specific application is scarcely unique to Web browsers: all personal computer operating systems need some mechanism for properly opening a data file when you click it.)

You can set up your browser's preferences for helper applications and plug-ins; you also can frequently set such preferences for your computer's desktop. In either case, you wind up with a collection of information that looks somewhat like that shown in Table 4-1. Not shown in this sample table are additional browser- and operating system-specific options that let you further refine your choices. (For example, you can choose to have a given data type saved to disk or displayed within a browser window.)

When a file is sent to your browser, the browser may look at a three-character suffix to determine what to do with it. In such cases, it uses the application shown in your preferences (such as listed in Table 4-1) to handle it. When data is included within an e-mail message or within the HTML of a Web page, it is typically identified with a MIME type such as the ones shown in Table 4-1. (Since included data is part of another data flow, it cannot have a file extension—the data flow may have several embedded types of data and may well have its own file extension.)

Helper applications for files are launched based on these file extensions and MIME types. They are triggered by the arrival of data either within an HTML page or as a separate file.

Description	Protocol/MIME Type	Suffix	Application
Excel Spreadsheet	application/vnd.ms-excel	.xls	Excel
Microsoft Word Document	application/msword	.doc	Microsoft Word
Microsoft Word Template	application/msword	.dot	Microsoft Word
PC Zip Archive	application/x-zip-compressed	.zip	ZipIt
Portable Document Format	application/pdf	.pdf	Acrobat Reader
PowerPoint Presentation	application/vnd. ms-powerpoint	.ppt	PowerPoint
Telnet	telnet	–	NCSA Telnet
Unix Tape Archive	application/x-tar	.tar	tar

TABLE 4-1. Sample Helper Application Preferences

While you can frequently launch helper applications on their own (as is the case with Microsoft Word), in other cases they only can be launched in response to the arrival of such data. In their role as helper applications, they only are launched in the latter way.

Protocol Helpers

Protocol helpers (such as the NCSA Telnet application shown in Table 4-1) help your browser manage protocols that it does not natively handle. Typical protocols are Telnet, Gopher, and other early Internet protocols. In some cases, custom protocols are supported by custom-written protocol helpers.

The difference between file helpers and protocol helpers is that file helpers act on a file after it has been received by the browser. Protocol helpers interact at the message level in a continuing flow of data between the browser and the remote server.

Scripts	Finally, scripts are written in a scripting language (such as VBScript, JScript, TCL, JavaScript, or Perl). They are typically distributed as text files, and are interpreted by the browser or server as needed. They are executed by that browser or server in its own memory partition.

They are often executed in response to events (just as applets and servlets are). They also can be executed directly by connecting a browser to their URL (provided that the browser can handle the scripting language in question—either natively or through a helper or plug-in).

Why This Matters for Application Servers	Odds are that you are not going to be writing an application server—or a database or a Web server (much less a Web browser). However, deploying application server-based solutions frequently involves writing and deploying software. This can be custom-written software that handles mission-specific issues, or it can be a collection of off-the-shelf products and reusable software components that interact with one another, the Web server, database, and application server.

The by-now familiar architecture of Web server–application server–database handles an enormous amount of the processing for these systems. Customization is necessary for the interface and for the specific database as well as for the business logic. It is necessary to understand the basic architecture to know what needs to be added to it: one of the most common problems is adding too much. The sub-programs that need to be written are often quite modest in scope.

Client-Side Programming

Client-side programming deals with programming at the user's computer; it is typically incorporated into a Web browser in one way or another. All of the three types of sub-programs can be used for client-side programming.

Client-side programming is typically used in the following ways:

- Interface enhancement
- Date entry editing
- Client integration

Interface Enhancement	The most common use of client-side programming is interface enhancement such as animating parts of a Web page as the mouse moves over them. This type of programming is often self-contained and may use stock routines. (It does not really matter what the image changes to when you move the mouse over it.)

Data Entry Editing	More complex than interface enhancement is data entry editing that is done with client-side programming. Scripts and applets can be used to perform validation for data entry fields. These validations can be as simple as ensuring that a field is not blank or as complex as determining that a value entered into a field is valid (and that particular validation may involve the sub-program's interacting with databases and programs on the user's computer).

Client Integration	The most complex type of client-side programming is that in which the script or applet is sent from the server and performs operations (such as data retrieval) on the user's computer. The simplest example of this type of programming is a client-side script that retrieves a cookie from the user's computer and uses the cookie information to create a message such as "Welcome back, Uta." A more complex example would do the same thing but would retrieve the information from a file or database on the user's computer.
Why This Matters	Client-side programming can extend a browser's functionality both graphically and with regard to the data that it displays. When you are designing systems that use application servers, it is frequently useful to place operations such as data validation on the client side to minimize network transmission and computation requirements.
	The downside to this is that client-side programming requires resources—not just computational resources, but also operational resources. Java must be present and enabled in order for Java applets to run; similarly, ActiveX objects require their own environment. If you are designing a system to be used in an enterprise where you control the environment, this is not a problem. However, if you are designing a system that will be used by a wide variety of people using different browsers with different configurations, this can be a serious issue.

Sometimes designers fail to understand that their specification of a "standard" environment is illogical. For the typical user—or employee—who does a variety of chores ranging from online banking to Web surfing to e-commerce, no standard environment can apply to all the tasks.

Server-Side Programming

Server-side programming is the complement to client-side programming: the sub-programs run on the server, and their results are presented as HTML that is downloaded to the user who basically has no awareness that any subprogram has been run. Server-side programming lies at the heart of application servers.

You do not have to worry about compatibility in the environment: you control the server's environment, so the decision of whether to enable Java, ActiveX, or other programming support tools is yours (or your ISP's). Server-side programming enables the server to communicate with other systems and computers to consolidate data (as from databases) in the HTML that is downloaded to the user.

The Interfaces

Exactly how does this work? How do subprograms on the server communicate with the Web server and vice versa? Standard protocols and interfaces have been designed to make this possible and to make the components portable across varying environments.

The goals of these interfaces are three-fold:

1. They enable the Web server to request that a subprogram run.

2. They provide a data structure whereby the Web server and the subprogram can share application-independent data (such as the version of the Web server that is being run).

3. They provide a mechanism for application-specific data to be transferred between the subprogram and the Web server.

The three primary interfaces are CGI, ISAPI, and NSAPI.

CGI

The oldest standard interface is the Common Gateway Interface (CGI). A CGI process is launched by the Web server and runs in its own address space; frequently, the process involves a Perl script which accesses the CGI data and performs necessary tasks. CGI is simple, straightforward, and sometimes inefficient for high-performance Web sites.

Although CGI is frequently used by Perl scripts and other interpreted languages, it can also be used from high-level languages such as C, C++, and Java.

ISAPI

The Internet Server Application Program Interface (ISAPI) is a set of Windows calls that you can access from a programming language. You write a Dynamic Linked Library (DLL) that uses ISAPI calls, and when necessary the DLL is called by the Web server (in its own address space). For this reason and because it is compiled (rather than interpreted as many CGI scripts are), it can be more efficient than the CGI interface.

As you can gather from the fact that ISAPI calls are Windows calls, this is a Windows-based implementation.

NSAPI

The Netscape Server Application Program Interface (NSAPI) is Netscape's high-level language interface. Unlike ISAPI, it provides support beyond the Windows environment.

Because ISAPI and NSAPI programs are compiled, they must be compiled for the specific operating system on which they are to run. By using conditional compilation directives, you can easily write multi-platform programs, but remember that unlike Perl scripts, you do need to recompile them.

The Protocols

The two basic protocols that make the Web happen are HTTP and HTML. They are described at length in *Database-Driven Web Sites*.

HTTP

Hypertext Transmission Protocol (HTTP) is the communications protocol for the Web. As such, it is comparable to e-mail, file transfer, and other protocols. HTTP is normally used to transmit Web pages—text files written in HTML.

In its official description,[1] HTTP is described as "an application-level protocol for distributed, collaborative, hypermedia information systems. It is a generic, stateless, object-oriented protocol which can be used for many tasks, such as name servers and distributed object management systems, through extension of its request methods. A feature of HTTP is the typing and negotiation of data representation, allowing systems to be built independently of the data being transferred."

Two points need to be made. The first is that HTTP's definition explicitly separates the data from the transfer mechanism; this compartmentalization is in keeping with the architecture that has evolved into application servers. The

---

1. HTTP is described in RFC 2068. You can find it in many places on the Web by searching for "RFC 2068."

second point is that HTTP is stateless—that is, after data is transferred, HTTP retains no trace of it, and the connection must be made anew for each transfer. Thus, transactions that involve several transfers—such as adding items to a shopping cart, refining searches that have previously been executed, and maintaining a password-enabled connection—must be implemented outside HTTP in application servers or databases.

HTML

Hypertext Markup Language (HTML) is a Structured Generalized Markup Language (SGML) that combines content with formatting information. Techniques such as cascading style sheets (CSS) and XML have been devised to structure this architecture more thoroughly; specifically, it is becoming increasingly important to separate formatting information (presentation commands) from descriptive information (commands that specify what the data is—name, address, etc.).

Web Servers and HTTP Servers

As noted previously, the term Web server is used to refer both to the computer that provides Web services as well as to the software (Apache, Microsoft Internet Information Server, Netscape Server, and so forth). For the balance of this book, a distinction will be made as follows:

- A Web server is the computer to which users connect and which provides Web pages on demand.

- An HTTP server is the software running on a Web server that serves up the pages (Apache, Microsoft Internet Information Server, Netscape Server, and so forth). In some cases, multiple HTTP servers run on a single Web server.

Summary

On the client side of the picture—in your browser—a variety of sub-programs are used to expand the functionality of basic HTML pages. These sub-programs come in three types:

1. Helper applications and plug-ins,

2. Applets and servlets, and

3. Scripts.

On the server side—in the Web server or application server—sub-programs also are used to expand functionality and to customize interactions with other systems. Here, what matters is the common interfaces—CGI, ISAPI, and NSAPI—that let a host of different types of software work with the servers.

The point of using subprograms with standard interfaces is to be able to expand and extend basic functionality of the HTTP and HTML protocols without having to rewrite Web servers and browsers from scratch. This standards-based system has evolved successfully over the years.

Recently, a more structured form of sub-programs has emerged. In the next chapter, you will see how object-oriented components are used on the server side.

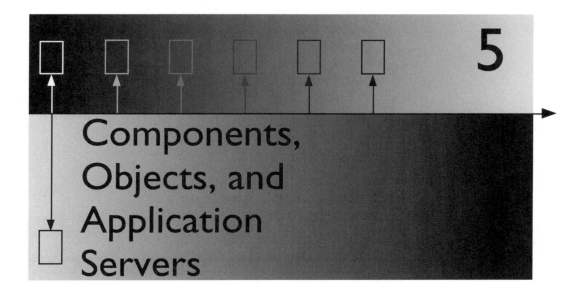

Components, Objects, and Application Servers

Application servers—like most software today—involve object-oriented technology in the form of components and objects. Components and objects are encapsulated and (ideally) reusable pieces of software that embody specific functionality and logic. Through well-defined interfaces, they are able to communicate between and among a variety of languages and computers. They can be assembled and reassembled in many ways without rewriting or recompiling their code. That, at least, is the goal.

In fact, this technology has settled down (somewhat) in the last few years to three often overlapping technologies: Microsoft's Component Object Model (COM) and its companion technologies from that company, Sun's JavaBeans and Enterprise JavaBeans, and the

Common Object Request Broker Architecture (CORBA) from the Object Management Group (OMG).

The varying architectures overlap in some ways: COM and CORBA have a defined interface (OMG's COM/CORBA Interworking Specification), Enterprise JavaBeans and CORBA are closely tied, and a variety of proprietary products for links and bridges between and among these components. Microsoft products tend to provide support only for COM and its associated technologies; other application server products provide support either for the other side of the fence (CORBA and/or Enterprise JavaBeans) or for all three technologies.

This chapter provides a brief overview of component technology in a distributed world.

Component and Object Technology History

Object-oriented programming began as a concept in which self-contained objects functioned on their own. Each object had functions or methods that carried out operations; furthermore, each object contained data (fields or properties). The object could act on its own data or on data passed into its functions or methods.

The variety of naming conventions reflects the broad background of component technology: Smalltalk, C++, Objective-C, and Java (among other languages).

As programmers and software architects began to actually use object-oriented technologies (starting in the late 1980s), several ways of working rose and fell.

| Frameworks | In order to write useful applications, it was necessary to develop objects to do all of the things that the applications needed to do. This was precisely the area in which object-oriented programming would appear to shine: common routines for printing, mouse tracking, window management, and so forth. And, in fact, that was the case. Large frameworks of object-oriented code were developed to handle all of these tasks. The developer of a new application needed just to insert application-specific code and voila: a full-blown application. |

The frameworks, however, quickly became quite big. The largest and most widely used of the early frameworks was Apple's MacApp, and its learning curve was notoriously steep and long. From Redmond, Microsoft Foundation Classes (MFC) emerged as a companion to MacApp in the Windows world. MetroWorks developed a third framework, PowerPlant, for the Mac OS; it used advanced object-oriented programming techniques (including extensive use of multiple inheritance).

The challenge in all cases was to achieve the savings promised by object-oriented programming techniques without burdening programmers with the task of learning an enormous "labor-saving" environment's rules and details.

| Objects in Non-Framework Environments | Meanwhile, the growth of the Web and HTML pages everywhere provided a different environment in which objects could function. Monolithic applications still exist, of course, but a very large number of Web-based applications also exist. These are HTML pages that contain text, graphics—and small objects that work in the controlled yet powerful environment of a Web page. In this way, the programmer is no longer faced with the need to understand an entire framework that can produce a self-contained application; instead, the program- |

mer can leave printing to a browser's default printing capabilities, can let the browser handle mouse tracking, and so forth.

Newer frameworks such as Enterprise JavaBeans have emerged in the last few years, but they are not designed primarily to enable programmers to create monolithic applications. The new breed of frameworks are designed to help programmers use object-oriented techniques to create objects—self-contained units of functionality—that can function within HTML pages or even within similarly defined environments in application programs (such as the Microsoft Office suite).

Components and Object Terminology

Objects consist of data and methods or functions. They are like little programs with very clearly defined interfaces for their input and output. Ideally, the internals of the object (or program) are hidden. You know that the object can compute its height, for example, but you do not know the mechanism that the object uses for this computation. This makes it easy to replace objects: their functionality (sometimes called business logic) is defined, but their implementation is private.

The key concepts in this architecture are

- classes;
- interfaces;
- objects and instantiations;
- how objects are manipulated; and
- the differences between components and objects.

Those concepts are discussed briefly in this section. In the next section, the critical implementation issue is discussed: how it all happens at run-time.

Classes	A class (sometimes called an object class) is a collection of methods, functions, or other routines that implement a single type of functionality. Hidden inside the class may be data elements that are used by the class's routines and that may be able to be set or retrieved via those routines.
Classes as Objects	The class itself may be an object, in which case it has certain routines that it can use to create instances of itself (see "Objects and Instantiations" starting on page 104). In some architectures, the class information is used as source material for a generalized routine that creates instantiations of the class.
Identification	A class must be identifiable in order to be used. In the case of distributed systems, it has a name that is globally unique in one way or another so that the class can be identified over a network. In that way, a program can request an instantiation of class XYZ and know that it is getting XYZ.

Interfaces	A class (or object class) has an interface which is the sum total of its functions, methods, or other routines. In some languages, this interface may have data elements, too.

In the best designed objects, no data elements are visible to the outside world: all data is accessed via functions (typically named with names such as GetCustomerID and SetCustomerID).

A class may have more than one interface. When a program deals with a concrete instantiation of the class, it may use one or another interface.

Objects and Instantiations

An object is an instantiation of a class (or object class). You can think of the class as a blueprint or plan: from it, individual houses, chairs, or other concrete objects can be created at will. A class may have data within it—much as a house plan may show shelves in a kitchen. Each actual object—analogous to each house built from the plan—has its own values for its data (its own collection of cans and boxes of various products).

There are cases in which the class itself has some data; the most obvious is that the class has an identifier. These may be called static variables, and there are a variety of ways in which to access the class variables from within instantiations of that class. For all practical purposes, you cannot access class data except through an instantiation of the class in the form of an object.

How Objects Are Manipulated

Objects can be used in a variety of languages; some of those languages are specifically designed for objects (C++, Objective C, Java, and J++ for example) while others predate the object model or simply ignore it to one degree or another (Cobol, C, and Perl for example).

Depending on the language that you use, you deal with an object via a pointer to a memory location or by a native language construct that is an object (at least as far as you are concerned). Java (which does not use memory pointers), uses the second method; in fact, everything in Java is an object so there is no need to specify a special way of working with objects.

The run-time instantiation of a class in the form of an object can happen in response to requests from programs written in a variety of languages. As a result, a standard interface to the class is usually provided; such an interface is written in an Interface Definition Language (IDL) which is designed to be used with a variety of programming languages (or which is able to be generated in a variety of programming languages).

Components Versus Objects	Although the terms object and component are sometimes used interchangeably, they have different meanings to purists. While exceptions can be found to every rule (including these), here is a brief checklist of differentiations between the two constructs.

- Components are often relatively large entities. Their purpose is frequently expressed in terms of business logic (as is the case with payroll system components, database management components, and so forth). They may consist of none, one, or more objects (nothing requires a component to be based on object-oriented design).

- Objects (which may be components or parts of components) are typically smaller entities. They come and go as processing proceeds, and a variety of copies of an object (instantiations), are frequently in use. (For example, a single payroll component may instantiate a separate employee object for each employee of the organization.)

- Following from the previous point, it is necessary that objects be able to contain state information and data that differentiate one instantiation from another.

- Similarly, components—which are typically not instantiated repeatedly in a given computer environment—do not contain stateful information.

Unfortunately, these distinctions have evolved over time with the growth of this technology, and they are not always strictly observed. Furthermore, some trademarked terminology (Microsoft Component Object Model springs to mind) muddles the distinction between components and objects. If you are relying on this set of distinctions, make certain that the people with whom you are conversing rely on the same distinctions.

How It Happens

The basic implementation of this technology is the same in all architectures. The objects are defined using an Interface Definition Language (IDL) which provides a language-neutral representation of each object's fields and methods. The IDL for each object (which is often generated automatically by development tools) is included in the program or subprogram that needs to use each object. Also included in the program are interface definitions and libraries that are needed to implement the object model being supported.

Objects that are defined and implemented locally—that is, within the given program or subprogram—may use a different implementation strategy. Such objects do not need to be shared and so the language-neutral IDL interface is not required; the object can be declared and implemented in the language of the program and that is the end of that.

Depending on the architecture and the implementation you are dealing with, how all this works may be quite object-oriented—or remarkably un-object-oriented. Early implementations of C++ used a precompiler (CFront) that converted all the nice object-oriented code and classes to plain old C code that did not have a whiff of objectivity about it.

What is important to note is that the implementation of the object model that you are using is basically compiled and/or linked into the programs that you write. Nice diagrams showing objects floating in space linked by arrows to programs on clients and servers do not generally suggest that those objects are actually part of the programs' runtime environment and that those arrow-linked bubbles do not exist outside of those programs.

What Matters About the Architectures

There are significant differences in the various architectures (most particularly between the COM architectures and those of CORBA and Enterprise JavaBeans). In practice, however, most applications do not use even a small fraction of the architectural features. The issue of multiple inheritance, for example, is theoretically of critical importance. In practice, complex hierarchies of inheritance rarely are implemented in most day-to-day systems. In comparing architectures, compare the features that you use and are likely to use: in most cases, the differences are not significant.

What is likely to be significant is performance, and in most cases, performance on comparable hardware is likely to be equal (this is, after all, a highly competitive world). Not only is performance likely to be comparable, but of all the variables affecting performance, the most potent—hardware—is ultimately the least expensive. Improving performance by using obscure programming tricks (or even not-so-obscure ones) is likely to be very expensive in both the short run and the long haul: the cost of programmers keeps going up, and the cost of computers keeps coming down.

This may be heresy to the purists and hogwash to the sales folk, but it is true.

There is one critical decision point that does matter, and that is what software you have installed, what development tools and skills you have, and what third-party products you use. If your environment consists of Windows NT, MTS is an option (as are CORBA and Enterprise JavaBeans). In a Unix world, MTS is not an option.

While it is not difficult to discover what computer you have on your desktop, it is not at all unusual in many organizations to have environments that are heterogeneous. The question then becomes not, "Do we run on Unix, Macintosh, Linux, Be, or Windows?" but "Do we run this new project on the Accounting System (Windows), the Research System (Unix), or the Human Resources System (Macintosh)?"

Summary

The world of application servers relies heavily on the highly structured and well-defined interfaces of components. This rigorous architecture lets products from various vendors (and from in-house programmers) work together harmoniously. To a large extent, the world of application servers represents the goal toward which programmers have been striving for decades in terms of interoperability and reuse of code.

The major component technologies involved in the world of application servers are COM/DCOM (from Microsoft), CORBA (from the Object Management Group), as well as Enterprise JavaBeans from Sun. This chapter has provided a general overview of this type of architecture. More details are provided later in Chapter 7, "Connecting to Logic: COM, CORBA, EJB, and RMI" starting on page 127.

This part of the book has provided a broad overview of the basic technologies that make application servers possible and on which they rely. The next part of the book goes more deeply into the technical issues of these technologies.

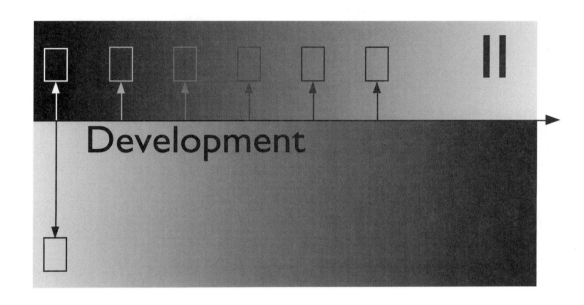

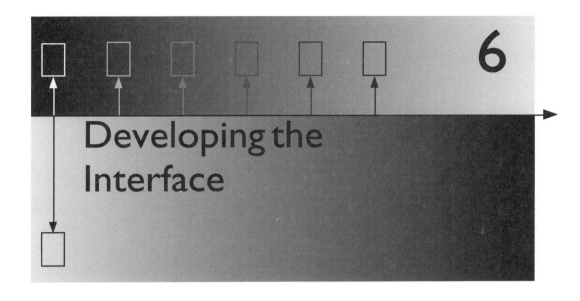

6

Developing the Interface

This part of the book provides an overview of the technologies that are used to implement the designs discussed previously. In particular, you will find in this chapter a discussion of small-scale objects (ActiveX controls and JavaBeans) that can be added to Web pages and executed by the user's browser; you will then find a discussion of larger-scale objects that can be added to Web page templates and descriptions and that are executed by the Web server (with their results downloaded to the user).

Finally, there is a brief discussion of XML (eXtensible Markup Language), Active Server Pages, and JavaServer Pages. XML is a major tool that makes developing and using Web pages even easier than be-

fore. ASP and JSP are technologies that automate the creation of Web pages. They often work in conjunction with application servers.

The following chapter goes even further up the scale of things: it discusses objects that run in application servers (and in other environments). These are the objects and components that typically use Microsoft's COM/DCOM technology, the cross-platform CORBA specification, or Sun's Enterprise JavaBeans architecture.

The third and final chapter in this part of the book looks at special-purpose objects and interface technology that are used to interact with databases.

The Key to Application Servers

The architecture described in Part I of this book evolved over time. The key step was when HTML pages were able to contain code that ran on the browser's machine. This code was originally designed primarily to animate and enhance the interface. Soon, however, programmers discovered that it provided a hook to remote computing resources.

If you think about it for a moment, the classic model described in this book has one major omission: how do you start programs running on the remote server? Everything in the Web design (both HTTP and HTML) is based on a request from a user and a response from the server. The request is for a resource identified by a URL; the response is typically a page of HTML text.

There are Web protocols that allow you to run programs on remote computers (Telnet is one such protocol). However, they come with some problems for many people. The structure that has evolved here allows a user to click on an interface element of a Web page (such as a button) and cause a program to start running on either the local computer or the remote

Web server. That is what is so important about the technology described in this chapter.

The problems involved in starting a program on a remote computer range from the simple issue of identifying the program and its computer to very complex issues of security. All of these issues are addressed (if not solved) with the technologies described in this chapter.

Furthermore, as soon as you can start a program running on a remote computer, that program can use similar technologies to start and communicate with programs on its own and other computers. The later chapters in this part of the book show how these technologies expand in this manner.

However, it all starts with embedding objects on Web pages—objects that enhance the interface and that incidentally (but very importantly) can do a variety of other tasks.

Adding Applets and ActiveX Controls to Web Pages on the Client

HTML provides the ability to incorporate many types of non-text information to Web pages (images being the most common). Early on, it became clear that a variety of other types of objects would need to be added over time. Rather than develop a separate syntax for each type of object, HTML (as of the 4.0 specification) has added the OBJECT element.

| The Object Element | The OBJECT element lets you specify the location and attributes of an object that is to be inserted into a Web page. The object may be an ActiveX control or a Java applet—or any of a variety of other objects (including images). The HTML OBJECT element can have a variety of attributes (they are listed |

below). The OBJECT element requires an end tag—that is, an </OBJECT> tag to follow the <OBJECT> tag. Between the two, text may be placed. It is displayed if the object in question cannot be retrieved. (In this way it is like the ALT attribute of the IMG element.)

The OBJECT element is discussed at length here because it is an addition to the HTML standard in HTML 4.0 and some of the techniques you may be familiar with will no longer be supported or encouraged.

IMG and APPLET Elements

Although the IMG element remains, the OBJECT element can provide a more generic means of inserting images onto a page; furthermore, it provides the only way of inserting some other types of objects.

Similarly, the APPLET element which is used only to insert Java applets onto HTML Web pages is deprecated in HTML 4.0 (its use is not encouraged and it will be removed from the syntax at some point in the future).

OBJECT Attributes

Any of the following attributes may be specified for an OBJECT element. You rarely use all—or even many—of these attributes for a single OBJECT. However, the scope of the attributes shows you the features that OBJECT elements can be expected to have or perform.

- **declare** You can specify that the object is to be downloaded but not actually instantiated. This is used for optimization in conjunction with the PARAM element and value attribute described later in this section.

- **classid** This is the URL of the object's code.

- **data** This is the URL of the object's data. This separation of code and data can provide efficiencies, particularly if one or the other is cacheable.

- **archive** A list (delimited by spaces) of URLs which may contain additional information needed for the object. Using this attribute can speed up load time, since the browser can make connections to these additional URLs as soon as possible.

- **codebase** This is used in conjunction with the **classid**, **data**, and **archive** attributes. It is the base path used to resolve URL references.

- **type** The type of data expected in the data attribute.

- **codetype** The type of data expected for the classid code. (The default is the same as the type attribute.)

- **standby** This is a string of text that can be displayed during the loading of code and data.

Other attributes that OBJECT elements have in common with other HTML elements are the following:

- **id**
- **class**
- **lang**
- **title**
- **style**
- **onclick, ondblclick, onmousedown, onmouseup, onmouseover, onmousemove, onmouseout, onkeypress, onkeydown,** and **onkeyup**
- **height**
- **width**
- **usemap**
- **name**
- **tabindex**
- **align**
- **border**
- **hspace** and **vspace**

PARAM Elements	Within the OBJECT element, you can include any number of PARAM elements. These provide run-time parameters to the object. There are five attributes for a PARAM element:

- **id**

- **name** This is the name that the object code expect to find.

- **value** This is the value for that name. (These are equivalent to the name/value pairs in query parts of URLs.)

- **valuetype** This detemines the type of the value attribute. Its possible values are **data** (in which case the value attribute's text is passed to the object), **ref** (a URL where the run-time data is stored), and **object** (in which case the value parameter is interpreted as the name of an object—possibly previously downloaded on this page).

- **type** For **ref** valuetypes. This is the type to be found at the URL.

Objects Versus Scripts

Finally, it is important to differentiate between objects and scripts. Scripts—such as PerlScript, JavaScript, Visual Basic, and so forth—are sections of code that are placed within the page and are executed by the browser as the page loads. Objects are located outside the Web page and are downloaded separately. They are executed by the browser—often indirectly, as when a Java applet is executed by a Java Virtual Machine.

A very important point to note about objects is that their code is downloaded in a binary or byte-code format; scripts normally are included in the Web page as text. The text is readable by anyone who understands the scripting language. Despite the presence of decompilers and other code-reading software, it is significantly more difficult to decipher binary or byte-code. This means that hackers and other unscrupulous individuals have a clear roadmap in front of them when a script is part of a Web page; executable objects pose more of a challenge.

| Why This Matters | The OBJECT element (like the APPLET element before it) provides the means to: |

The OBJECT element (like the APPLET element before it) provides the means to:

- Download executable code from a location on the Web,

- Execute it, and

- Pass parameters into it either from the Web page itself or from a location on the Web.

In other words, it allows you to run a small program (or applet) from a Web page. The program is executed when the Web page loads (unless you set DECLARE=TRUE).

What the program does is up to the author of the program and the rules of the language in which it is written. (Java applets, for example, run in a "sandbox"—they do not have access to all of a computer's resources. ActiveX controls, however, can do just about anything thing they want to on your computer.)

Types of Objects

The two major types of applets you will find in use today are ActiveX controls and Java applets. Both were initially developed primarily to provide graphical enhancements to a Web page. Today, both are used for other purposes, including accessing databases, editing data, and communicating with application servers.

ActiveX Controls

ActiveX controls were initially designed simply to enhance the user interace. They can be used in Visual Basic, Microsoft Office, and, of course, on Web pages. There are three aspects to ActiveX Controls that are of significance:

1. writing ActiveX Controls,

2. how to use them on Web pages and in Visual Basic scripts, and

3. what happens at run time when the user activates them.

You may recognize some of this technology. ActiveX controls used to be OLE controls or OCX controls; before that, they were VBXs.

Writing ActiveX Controls

ActiveX controls can be written in C or C++ as well as Visual Basic and Microsoft Visual J++. You may need to know about OLE or COM/DCOM, but using templates or examples as your starting point can help you get up to speed quickly.

Using (not writing) ActiveX controls—either as an end-user or as the author of a Web page—normally does not require any of this knowledge.

ActiveX controls are often downloaded as part of Web pages. In order to maintain a degree of security, the controls need to be signed and marked. Signing guarantees who has written the control; marking provides information about what it can (and cannot do).

Signing ActiveX Controls

ActiveX controls support a signing mechanism in which a trusted third party provides a digital signature that is downloaded as part of the control. That digital signature states the verified signer of the control (in other words, if it is says that it was signed by Queen Victoria, that is who actually signed it). This enables you to know who you are dealing with when an ActiveX control is downloaded to a Web page.

The fact that ActiveX controls are used and reused many times means that the owner of the Web page may not be—and often is not—the author of the ActiveX control.

Marking ActiveX Controls

In addition to a signature, ActiveX controls can be marked with either of two safety levels (or neither):

1. **Safe to initialize** means that no value for any parameter in the control can be set that will cause damage. (For example, if the control computes a ratio, supply 0 as a denominator will not cause a divide-by-zero error.)

2. **Safe to script** means that you can write a script that accesses any of the control's interface methods and nothing that any of them can do can cause damage. Operations that could cause damage include certain interactions with the file system or registry, some memory manipulations, the lack of input data validation, and so forth.

How Signatures and Marks Are Implemented

It is not sufficient to sign and mark your controls: users need to set appropriate levels of security in their browser preferences. You can turn off all security—this means that signatures and markings are ignored; alternatively, you can set a very high level of security where if signatures are not present or appropriate markings not in place, the controls are simply ignored. Intermediate levels of security are available.

Note that while the signatures are verified by a trusted third party, developers are responsible for the safety markings on their controls. Errors (and sometimes deliberate misleading information) can creep into these markings in this way.

Why This Is Necessary

This is necessary because ActiveX controls have the run of your computer—they can essentially do anything. Some malignant controls have been created; more frequently, controls designed for a single benign purpose have been reused for another benign purpose—but the lack of testing in the second case has left a vulnerability (or bug) exposed.

Java applets (described in the following section), provide a different approach to this issue. As you will see, they do not have the run of the computer—they must stay in a "sandbox." Since they cannot perform certain types of operations, it is not necessary to mark them.

Authoring with ActiveX Controls

Many ActiveX controls can be downloaded to a Visual Basic or JavaScript development environment and manipulated graphically. Some more sophisticated controls may require that you actually write a small amount of scripting code to interact with the control.

You can use the ActiveX Control Pad to insert ActiveX controls into Web pages that you are designing.

ActiveX Controls on Web Pages

The browser uses the information in the OBJECT element to determine whether or not an ActiveX control is available on the user's system. (The globally unique class ID is used for this purpose.) If it is not, it uses additional information in the OBJECT element to locate the control and to download it. The signature and markings described previously are used in conjunction with the browser's security preference to properly handle the controls.

JavaBeans and Java Applets

Java applets can be incorporated into Web pages using the OBJECT element in the same way as ActiveX controls can be. (The now-deprecated APPLET element can also be used.) The biggest distinction between ActiveX controls and Java applets and JavaBeans is that Java applets and JavaBeans are written in Java and ActiveX controls are written in a variety of languages. In addition, like ActiveX controls, Java applets can have digital signatures attached so that the user can determine their origin. However, since applets are limited in what they can do, the marking of ActiveX controls as to their intentions within the environment is not provided.

JavaBeans are also similar to ActiveX controls (although the fiercest partisans of each technology would deny even the remotest similarity).

JavaBeans are reusable software components that are designed to be manipulated in a graphical development tool—just as ActiveX controls are. One of the biggest differences between the ActiveX world and the world of Java is that in the ActiveX world, the components tend to be bigger, more powerful, and to run primarily on Windows operating systems. In the Java world, the components tend to be smaller, more focused, and to run on a wide variety of operating systems. Each attribute can be (and is) a topic of wild disputation. Given the widespread use of both technologies (and the ease with which bridges can be built between them), it is unlikely that these arguments will end soon.

| JavaBeans and Java Applets | Applets are most often placed on Web pages. Within an applet (which is written in Java), a JavaBean can be used. You instantiate it and then call its methods as you see fit. (Both JavaBeans and ActiveX controls normally live within applets, scripts, or graphical environments.) |

Both ActiveX controls and JavaBeans can live within server-side environments such as scripts running on Web servers or Java servlets (applets running on a server).

| JavaBeans Features | An additional difference between the two worlds is that the ActiveX world tends to be more practical—that is, it sometimes appears that the architecture follows the implementation. Java—like CORBA—starts from a design and a reference implementation. Many people believe that it is more structured. |

It certainly is true that the JavaBeans API makes it very clear what beans can do:

- **Introspection**. A bean can report about how it works so that the development tool in which it is placed can help the designer use the bean.

- **Customization**. A bean's appearance and behavior can be overridden.

- **Events**. Beans communicate via events.

- **Properties**. Beans contain properties which can be accessed by programmers and which can be customized.

- **Persistence**. Beans can be saved and restored—along with customizations that may be added.

Note that while these features provide value to the ultimate user, they are primarily of importance to the Web page author who is using the bean. What the beans actually do is up to the bean developer.

JavaBeans Fundamentals	In addition to the basic features described in the previous section, several fundamental aspects of JavaBeans are worth noting since they affect the way in which you develop and use them.[1]
No Base Class	JavaBeans start from scratch: they do not descend from a base class or common interface. You can provide the functionality that you need and no more. (If the bean is visible, however, it must inherit from java.awt.Component.)
Design Environment versus Run-Time Environment	Beans must be able to run in at least two different environments. When a bean runs in a builder tool, it runs in a design environment. In such an environment, its introspection facilities allow a user to customize its appearance and behavior. When a bean runs in a run-time environment (as on a Web page) it carries out the actions that its designer has implemented (and that a designing user may have customized).
JavaBeans Run Inside Containers	Beans run inside containers; they do not have their own address spaces. Two common types of containers may be used. If a bean is part of a Java application, it runs in the same Java virtual machine as its container. On the other hand, if a bean is contained within a non-Java application, it will run in the Java virtual machine that is associated with that application. That machine may or may not be in the same address space as the application.
JavaBeans in a Distributed Environment	Beans are often used as front ends to remote data sources and other distributed resources. They normally do not implement their own connectivity. Rather, they use one of the three primary network access mechanisms available to developers:

---

1. For even more on this topic, see Chapter 2, "Fundamentals" of the JavaBeans API specification. It is available on the Web at http://java.sun.com/beans

1. **Java RMI**. Remote Method Invocation allows calls to be made to a remote server provided that it supports RMI.

2. **Java IDL**. This system implements the CORBA distributed object model. This is the pathway for beans to communicate to other technologies.

3. **JDBC**. This is the mechanism for beans to access SQL databases.

Adding Applets and ActiveX Controls to Web Pages on the Server

In addition to incorporating applets and controls on Web pages for the browser to handle, you can place applets and controls on Web pages at the server side. Instead of executing as the page is loaded, they execute as the page is created and before it is downloaded.

Such applets and controls are frequently used for interacting with other systems and with databases; they also are often used for calculations and computations. Whereas client-side applets and controls are often used for interface elements, server-side applets and controls are not. In fact, server-side applets and controls should have no visible interface (who would see it—the Web server operator?).

eXtensible Markup Language (XML)

XML is a language that builds on SGML (Standard Generalized Markup Language)—the underpinnings of HTML

Whereas HTML provides a way of formatting pages, XML provides a way of not only formatting the appearance of pages but also of describing their contents.

This solves a number of thorny problems. For example, when data is retrieved from a database and formatted into HTML, it can look very good, but it has lost its description. The table cell containing Name information is indistinguishable from that containing Address. With XML, the logical characteristics of the data can be preserved on the page—and on its subsequent travels through other systems. Because of its rapid and widespread adoption, XML is becoming another lingua franca of the Web.

From the start, the use of standards-based technologies has been critical to the growth of the Web and the Internet itself. By clearly delineating standards, protocols, and the roles that different types of software products can play, the world of application servers is made possible.

Active Server Pages and JavaServer Pages

As you saw in the diagrams in the first part of this book, application servers routinely generate HTML pages to be sent back to users. Active Server Pages (ASP) and JavaServer Pages (JSP) are dynamically created HTML pages that can be generated by Web servers. ASP technology is a Microsoft product, and primarily is available on Windows. JSP is a cross-platform technology.

In both cases, a script or Java code is run to dynamically create an HTML page. Since it is created dynamically, the page can include data that is calculated or retrieved by the script or code. Generating such a page happens when the user requests an HTML that ends with .asp or .jsp; that page generation may trigger substantial processing by an application server and/or database—or it may trigger nothing more dynamic than a script that inserts today's date on the page.

As you can see, the need (and desire) for dynamically created Web pages is growing, and there are many ways to fulfill these needs. ASP and JSP can be used on a small scale, or they can be integrated with application servers.

Summary

In this chapter you have seen how ActiveX controls and Java applets (together with JavaBeans) can extend both a browser and a Web server. The extensions to the browser and Web server are limited only by the imagination of the designer and the resources of the environment.

What is most important, however, is that controls and applets provide the hook through which other applications can run and through which data can flow into and out of other processes. It is in this way that a user with a browser can cause a database query to be run or a credit card transaction to be processed. This is the architecture that makes application servers work.

Communicating with those other processes requires standard interfaces. The next chapter goes on to explore COM/DCOM and CORBA—mechanisms for letting objects communicate with one another.

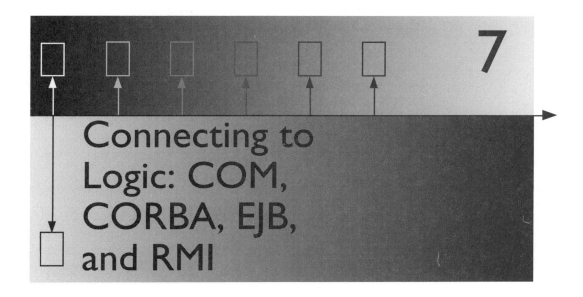

Connecting to Logic: COM, CORBA, EJB, and RMI

7

The component models that are widely used today fall into three categories that are not totally distinct. The first is the COM/DCOM technology (Microsoft's Component Object Model and Distributed Component Object Model). The second is the Object Management Group's Common Object Request Broker Architecture (CORBA). The third is the Enterprise JavaBean (EJB) architecture.

COM/DCOM is an implementation and an architecture that is implemented primarily by Microsoft; CORBA is an architecture that is implemented by a variety of vendors.

The ActiveX component architecture is the COM/DCOM framework for creating reusable components; the CORBA world does not have a comparable component architecture. However, the world of

Java (which is allied in many ways with CORBA), has JavaBeans—its own component architecture. (ActiveX and JavaBeans are discussed in "Developing the Interface" starting on page 111.)

Just to make things interesting, the Enterprise JavaBeans architecture relies on CORBA for many of its functions, but it is not strictly speaking a CORBA implementation. Furthermore, Java's Remote Method Invocation (RMI) system provides a means for objects to be invoked across a network, and it has certain functional overlaps with COM/DCOM and CORBA.

What Matters—and What Does Not Matter

Before delving into these architectures and implementations, you should note that the architectures are not mutually exclusive. In many cases, you are not required to take sides in what is sometimes a very ugly battle: COM/DCOM objects can interact with CORBA objects (in fact, a specific interworking protocol exists to this end). Just as with databases, the differences between architectures and products are frequently significant, but they often do not actually matter much in the real world. Choosing between one architecture and another is important—but it rarely is the single critical decision in a project.

Focus on the Business Logic

The business logic that your objects and components will represent is the most valuable part of any system you develop, and that business logic can usually be expressed in any architecture. The architecture-specific details often have more to do with deployment of a system, and while the deployment details differ, they are comparable. After all, each architecture must provide you with a way to produce an object, access its functionality, store it (sometimes) away, and restore it from its storage location. Focus not on what a given object model can or cannot do (they all can do almost anything that you want them to), but on what you need to do. Furthermore, if you are sitting with 50,000 lines of code expressing your business logic, remember that most likely the business logic is expressed at a much higher level than bits and bytes—and as such can easily be translated from one environment to another by someone who understands the business.

Lighten Up

If you can keep your sense of humor intact, it is even possible (albeit not in public) to find much that is amusing in the ongoing object-religion battle. Microsoft is determined to prove that its COM technology was "the original object component technology," while backers of CORBA hasten to point out that features of COM+ scheduled for release in Windows 2000 (formerly known as Windows 5.0) are essential to its operation, and that no matter what was introduced in 1993, there still is no practical COM architecture. On the other hand, CORBA's insistence that COM's implementation hides the fact that its architecture is flawed can be considered as risible since in fact COM-based—as well as CORBA-based—software is running successfully today.

Layers and Isolation

For several decades now, software architectures have been created in layers, with each layer responsible for a different aspect of functionality. The Internet's TCP/IP protocol consists of seven layers ranging from the physical connection between two computers to the software-only interaction between two programs. This approach helps to keep the most changeable and valuable part of an application—the business logic—independent of hardware.

The component models discussed in this chapter use layered approaches to their functionality; there are at least three major layers:

- A transport protocol—sometimes called a **wire protocol**—is used to implement the basic communications.

This wire protocol frequently is the Remote Procedure Call (RPC) specification in the Distributed Computing Environment (DCE) from the Open Group.[1]

- A middle layer lets the COM/DCOM or CORBA libraries talk to one another.

- The application or business logic layer consists of user-written code.

As in most layered architectures, each layer relies on the ones below it, and no layer needs to be aware of layers above it. Thus, as a writer or designer of business logic, you need not worry about how the transport layers are implemented.

Why This Matters	It is unusual for a system to be built around an application server: it is usually built around existing business systems. Those systems may use any (or all) of the technologies described in this chapter. The choice of an application server may be determined by the component models that already exist in an organization's inventory of software products.

COM/DCOM

Introduced on the desktop in 1993 and in a distributed version in 1996, COM is widely used on Windows as well as on some Unix and IBM mainframe systems. COM/DCOM is an integral part of Windows, and in many cases it is hard to separate it out.

---

1. http://www.opengroup.org/dce/introduction.htm

Overview

Compared to CORBA, COM/DCOM development often involves more lines of code; that is because the CORBA architecture contains a number of features that need to be explicitly written in COM/DCOM. This gives rise to fierce battles about which is harder to learn: CORBA (because you have to learn the architecture before you write a single line of code) or COM/DCOM (because you have to write so much more code). However, as noted previously, for most purposes, the two architectures both do what you need them to do. Furthermore, there are interworking standards to let you bridge the gap.

COM/DCOM was developed in the Windows world; it is part of Windows as it is deployed, and there is nothing extra to buy or install in most cases. (Whether or not that makes it "free" is up to economists and marketing experts to determine.)

COM components can be created in Java, Microsoft Visual C++, Microsoft Visual Basic, Delphi, PowerBuilder, Micro Focus Cobol, and a variety of other languages. As is the case with other components, the code you write is supplemented by code in various libraries and parts of the operating system (usually Windows); this code implements the transport and middle layers of functionality.

As a programmer, you use an interface pointer to manipulate a COM/DCOM object. You dereference that point as you would in C. The COM/DCOM system design is a binary standard; when you call the method of an object, you actually get a reference to that method from a vtable just as you would in C++. (vtables are virtual tables containing pointers to functions.)

If you don't understand this, don't worry. Just as with CORBA and with Enterprise JavaBeans, there are ways to refer to COM/DCOM object and ways to call their methods. Some people are very concerned about the ways in which these functionalities are implemented. If you are, you do understand this. If not, just forge ahead and do what you want to do.

IUnknown

As in many object-oriented systems, there is a base conceptual object from which others descend. In COM/DCOM, it is IUnknown, which is actually an interface. Since all COM/DCOM objects extend the IUnknown interface, all have its three methods, and all COM/DCOM objects implement these methods as well as their own. A look at those three methods shows a lot about the COM/DCOM architecture.

QueryInterface()

Objects may have multiple interfaces in COM/DCOM. Each interface consists of a set of methods. In order to call a method of an object, you must first obtain a pointer to the interface in question. You do this by calling QueryInterface—a method of IUnknown, and therefore a method of all COM/DCOM objects. Each interface has a unique universal identifier (a constant) which you pass into QueryInterface. You also pass in a pointer—which is returned as NULL if the interface does not exist. If the interface does exist, you can access its methods through the pointer.

This architecture quickly becomes second nature to you as you work with COM/DCOM objects; it can easily handle changes to interfaces as well as multiple interfaces to an object.

AddRef()

In any system that uses shared objects, there is alway a question of how to deal with destruction of those objects. While simple variables disappear at the end of a block of code, an object has a life beyond the block in which it is created—especially because if it is shared, it may have been created in a block in another program.

One way of handling this is to implement a reference count in each object. Whenever a program obtains a reference to an object, that reference count is incremented by 1. When a program is finished with an object, the reference count is decremented. (If 15 different programs on 15 different computers have simultaneous references to a single object, its reference count is 15.) The AddRef() method should be called as soon as you obtain a reference to an object; it is called automatically in many object creation routines.

Release()

If you use a reference count structure, you must call a Release() method when you are finished with an object. Release() decrements the reference count, and when it drops below 1, the object is deleted (since no references remain to it).

In a shared environment that uses this architecture, it is critical that both AddRef() and Release() be called in pairs. If they are not called properly, objects will be deleted while references to them are still active or they will clutter up memory long after their usefulness has faded.

Pings

There is a problem with this type of architecture, particularly when it is implemented across a network. If the remote process fails (or the network crashes), communication between the objects is obviously lost. If it is the server end of the link that fails (that is, where the object actually is located), any clients that attempt to use the object will be unable to do so. If a client fails, then calls to the object—including Release() calls—will not go through. As a result, you may have an object lying around with a reference count suggesting that it is in use when in fact its clients are no longer viable.

DCOM implements a pinging mechanism in which the computers and processes involved send pings ("hello" messages) to one another at periodic intervals. If the pings are not returned, then DCOM assumes a network or process failure and takes appropriate actions with regard to objects and references that may be affected.

HResult

Most COM/DCOM methods return a result code of type HResult. It is a 32-bite error code that lets you know what has happened during the method call. One important consequence of this architecture is that methods or functions always return a result code; any returned values are returned as parameters.

An IErrorInfo object is available to convert HResult into exceptions which are handled in a more sophisticated manner. (See "Exceptions" starting on page 139).

Client-Server Terminology

In a distributed world, shared components can be viewed in the client-server architecture. One component—the client—is referred to by one or more clients. In its implementation, DCOM uses the terms proxy and stub for these purposes. (This terminology is important because it differs from the CORBA terminology but overlaps and contradicts it in one case.)

Proxy

A proxy object is an object on the client that appers to be the remote object. (The remote object, of course, is located far away on the server computer.) One of the design considerations of COM/DCOM is to make the distance disappear. To use a distant object, you create an interface pointer to a proxy object and treat it basically as if it were a local object.

Stub

An object which is made available to clients has a stub. That stub (on the server) communicates with proxy objects (on clients). This communication is done largely by implementing the Remote Procedure Call (RPC) specification in the Distributed Computing Environment (DCE).

Service Control Managers

Service Control Managers (SCMs) on both the client and server computers are used to locate and activate implementations of objects. The method CoCreateInstance and its companion methods are used to create interface pointers to objects.

Those methods call the SCMs on the client and appropriate server computers; through their operations, the appropriate RPC link is set up and the proxy object (client) and stub are created and attached to that link. Thereafter, communication is directly between the proxy object and the stub—or, from the programmer's point of view, directly between the two objects.

Identification

COM/DCOM relies heavily on registries that contain unique identifiers for interfaces (interface IDs—IIDs), classes (class IDs—CLSIDs), and other aspects of the architecture. These unique identifiers are globally unique identifiers (GUIDs) that include a hardware address, a time stamp, a random component, and other information. They are generated automatically from these components and are, truly, unique.

In fact, the use of GUIDs within documents has proved to be problematic. Microsoft Office products incorporate a GUID in some of their documents, allowing them to be traced to a specific originating computer. This is considered to be a possible invasion of privacy. However, the Melissa virus that emerged in the spring of 1999 included such a GUID that enabled law enforcement authorities to relatively quickly locate the person who had created the virus. This area remains one of great interest, but the integrity of the GUID seems not to be in question.

Since registries are used to track these identifiers, changes to those registries can be made to modify the actual location of objects. This means that you can reconfigure a distributed system without any recompilation of code.

| Creating Objects | There are a number of ways of creating objects, but a common one is to include the IClassFactory object in an object's hierarchy alongside IUnknown. Methods of IClassFactory that can be used to create objects are: |

- CoCreateInstance
- CoGetInstanceFromFile
- CoGetInstanceFromStorage
- CoGetClassObject
- CoGetClassObjectFromURL

As you can tell from their names, you are able to deal with object persistance—restoring an object and its data from a file or other storage device. You can also call CoCreateInstance to create an uninitialized instance of an object; this is an important distinction between COM/DCOM and CORBA: CORBA allows object creation to include initialization (that is, the methods that create objects can take parameters).

CORBA

Despite the fact that both COM/DCOM and CORBA provide very similar functionalities, there are some fundamental differences that are crucial (although they may have minimal impact on your system designs). Both architectures involve the use of objects across space—in distributed systems. Corba, however, involves the use of objects across time—enabling you to use the same object today, tomorrow, and next week. (In COM/DCOM, each time you connect to an object you have a new identifier in the form of an object reference pointer.)

Despite this enormous difference (and it is enormous), you may find the effect on you and your operations to be minimal. Many objects have relatively brief life spans—the length of a single e-commerce transaction, for example. Even those objects that are persistent (a customer object, for example), can be reconstituted from files or other data stores in the COM/DCOM world. Remember that both architectures are used to power a wide variety of systems: if either architecture were unable to support e-commerce, online searching, dynamic Web sites, or some other application, the world would know it—and the other architecture's authors would be scribbling night and day to make it happen.

In fact, this is a fairly good summary of exactly what is happening. Someone— perhaps a marketing type—discovers something that can be done only in one architecture or which can be done significantly better in that architecture. Publicity ensues and late-night scribbling follows, and soon everyone can do everything. As noted constantly in this section, the really unique types of applications are few and far between.

Overview

The heart of CORBA is an Object Request Broker (ORB) which manages objects across time and space. Just as libraries and shared code in COM/DCOM implement the calls between objects, so libraries—in this case CORBA libraries—are compiled into CORBA applications or are available as run-time linked libraries. Calls from a client process to an object that runs in a server process are mediated by the ORB.

It is important to note that the ORB is an architectural concept: you will not find an ORB running on a computer. It is implemented with libraries and common routines within CORBA applications.

This is a very big deal to people who are strong partisans of one architecture over the other. COM/DCOM is "simpler" and "more efficient" because objects communicate directly with one another; CORBA is "more scalable" and "more robust" because of the intermediation of the ORB.

ORBs are written by a variety of vendors to the CORBA specification. ORBs can communicate with one another—the Internet Inter-ORB Protocol (IIOP) specifies a TCP/IP-based mechanism for this based on the General Inter-ORB Protocol (GIOP).

CORBA::Object	The base object in CORBA is CORBA::Object. It has a more methods than does IUnknown in COM/DCOM. A few of the major ones are described in this section.
get_interface()	Like IUnknown, there is a method that returns an interface definition. Unlike IUnknown, however, this is not a pointer that you use to reference the object's methods: it allows you to examine the interface and determine which methods to call.
duplicate() and release()	This pair of methods is used to create and then release copies of references to the object. Unlike COM/DCOM's AddRef() and Release() methods, however, these methods act only on references; the object itself is not affected. (In other words, calling release() will never cause the object to be freed.)
is_nil () and non_existent()	These methods let you test if an object exists or not. In COM/DCOM, these tests are unnecessary because (supposedly) all non-nil object reference pointers point to actual objects. If they do not, the reference counting and pinging structures most likely have failed. CORBA does not rely on those structures—ORBs are responsible for object maintenance. Therefore it is possible for you to check for a condition that apparently could not exist in COM/DCOM.
is_equivalent()	This method takes an object as a parameter and returns true if the ORB believes that that object is the same as the object

whose method is called. In the COM/DCOM world, pointers to interfaces and classes proliferate; in the CORBA world the unique identity of an object over time and space is important.

Exceptions

In many object-oriented languages today, a more sophisticated architecture is used to handle error conditions than the return codes used in COM/DCOM. Instead of returning a result code and checking it each time, the C++ try/catch exception mechanism (or a variation thereof) is employed.

In that structure, you set up a block of code which will succeed or fail as a unit (the try block). If it fails, another block of code (the catch block) is executed. It cleans up loose ends and may post error messages for a user. Exceptions are raised with a throw statement—which can include a specification of what the exception is. (Catch blocks often include handlers for specific types of exceptions.)

There is a final parameter in all CORBA method definitions—a pointer to an environment structure. This structure (which need not be explicitly specified in each method definition) is passed through the system; when an exception is thrown, it can provide information to help the ORB and the CORBA libraries in your software to identifiy and recover from the failure.

Client-Server Terminology

Like DCOM, CORBA has a client-server set of terminology. Unfortunately, it is not quite the same.

Stub/Proxy

The client program maintains a reference to the remote object. This reference takes the form of a client stub or proxy (both terms are used).

Skeleton	The server software maintains a representation of the object that will be shared with clients; that representation is called a skeleton.

In the DCOM world, the server representation of the shared object is called a proxy—one of the terms for the client-side object in CORBA.

Identification	Within a given ORB, object identifiers adhere to that ORB's naming convention. Across ORBs, the Interoperable Object Reference (IOR) structure is used. Rather than relying on globally unique identifiers, CORBA relies on a structure in which communicating ORBs manage their own identifiers and in turn negotiate the bridges between them. This mechanism—developed initially in IBM's Standard Object Model (SOM)—is scalable and arguably more robust than the COM/DCOM structure.

Creating Objects	Finally, the creation of CORBA objects is done by ORBs, not through a class factory method as is the case with COM/DCOM. This is rarely a significant issue, however, since in both cases your application code is able to request that an object be created and to get a reference to it.
	What does matter, however, is that ORBs can respond to a request to return an object by finding that object wherever it may be (on disk, in another ORB, or wherever) and returning it. The distinction between created by uninitialized objects and initialized objects that COM/DCOM permits is not possible with the CORBA architecture in most cases. (This, too, can be fodder for discussion about whether this makes CORBA more elegant or COM/DCOM more efficient.)

RMI

Java's Remote Method Invocation (RMI) system allows objects on one Java virtual machine to interact with objects on another Java virtual machine.

RMI/JRMP

RMI comes in two flavors. Its original implementation uses the Java Remote Method Protocol (JRMP), which was designed specifically for RMI. Using this flavor (abbreviated RMI/JRMP), you can handle the implementation of systems based on a variety of computers.

RMI/IIOP

The second version of RMI uses the Internet Inter-ORB Protocol (IIOP) and is abbreviated RMI/IIOP. Since IIOP is a standard protocol that can be used for communication between and among CORBA objects, you can use RMI/IIOP to interact not only with other Java objects but with objects written in languages other than Java.

Enterprise JavaBeans

Object-oriented programming in general and the object models discussed previously in this chapter have increasingly provided an environment in which only application-specific business logic needs to be written afresh for each new project. The protocols and frameworks perform more and more of the routine tasks. This has several consequences:

- New applications can be written more easily.

- More complex applications can be developed than would otherwise be possible.

- The standardization of routine tasks has led to the environment in which application servers can thrive. Idiosyncratic approaches to everything from input/output to user interfaces are becoming increasingly expensive to develop and maintain.

Enterprise JavaBeans is a server component model that goes even further. Together with the other Enterprise Java APIs, it provides standard objects and interfaces that can be used in a vendor- and technology-neutral world. That portion of an application that is truly unique (the business logic) is even smaller than it was before.

These APIs sometimes encapsulate a single technology—for example, the Java Transaction Service defines a distributed transaction management service that is based on CORBA's Object Transaction Service. In other cases, the APIs encapsulate functionality that can be provided in a variety of ways. The JDBC Database Access API, for example, provides a single interface that allows access to databases such as Oracle, SQL Server, Sybase, DB2, and Informix; the Java Naming and Directory Interface (JNDI) allows access to a variety of such services such as DNS, NDS, NIS+, LDAP, and COS Naming.

Enterprise JavaBeans use the RMI system (discussed in the previous section) for communications. Note that through RMI/IIOP, Enterprise JavaBeans can communicate with CORBA objects.

Two aspects of Enterprise JavaBeans give a flavor of the whole: the services that are provided to enterprise beans and the roles that can be played by individuals and organizations in the Enterprise JavaBeans world.

Enterprise JavaBeans Services	COM/DCOM objects as well as CORBA object have methods that provide basic and generalized services to those objects. Those methods involve issues such as creation, identification, and persistence.

Enterprise JavaBeans provide five services to their objects; these services show the functionalities that enterprise beans are expected to perform. Like all JavaBeans, enterprise beans are placed within containers. The container provides these services:

1. Lifecycle management, including allocation, activation, and destruction.

2. State management between method calls.

3. Security including user authentication and authorization.

4. Transaction support including rollback and commitment.

5. Persistence of data in a database.

Enterprise JavaBeans Roles	The Enterprise JavaBeans specification envisions six players in the creation and deployment of enterprise beans:

1. An Enterprise Bean Provider creates the enterprise beans that do the business-specific work. The bean provider must understand what the beans must do and how they must do it. An Enterprise Bean Provider can be a sophisticated end-user, a programmer who supports end-users, a vendor of domain-specific beans, or a consultant.

2. An Application Assembler combines enterprise beans with other components (such as Web pages) to create an application. This person need not understand how a bean does what it does, but does need to understand what it does.

3. The Deployer installs the enterprise beans. A deployer is typically part of an organization's IT staff.

4. An Enterprise JavaBeans Server Provider provides the software that supports the beans. These entities are typically vendors of application servers, databases, or operating systems.

5. Logically distinct from the previous entity, the Enterprise JavaBeans Container Provider provides container support. In practice today, application servers, databases, and operating systems provide both Server and Container support.

6. Finally, a System Administrator manages the ongoing operation and maintenance of the application. Typically, this is also a function of an organization's IT staff.

Note that only the first two entities need to understand the business logic. Application servers in general provide an architecture that helps to separate business logic from operational issues, but the Enterprise JavaBeans model takes this even further.

Types of Enterprise JavaBeans

Two types of Enterprise JavaBeans exist: session and entity beans.

Session beans manage transactions. They live for the duration of the user's session (whatever that may be).

Entity beans manage data within a database. They persist for the duration of the data's existence—perhaps for weeks or months. (This persistence is managed by Enterprise Java-Beans; they may be stored or cached for substantial periods of time during this period.)

The combination of session and entity beans lets you manage business logic at a totally object-oriented and abstracted level.

Interfaces

Each Enterprise JavaBean must have at least two interfaces. The remote interface is the interface that a client can call on a bean. The home interface is the interface that a server can call on that bean; it contains the construction, destruction, and lookup calls. Enterprise JavaBeans live on the server, but through their remote interfaces, clients can call them as needed.

Summary

The component models discussed in this chapter have more in common than their fiercest partisans would admit. The point of providing this overview is to show you what they do and how they do it. Remember that the underlying goal of these technologies is to reuse code as well as the analysis and design that underpin it. It is neither economically feasible nor useful to write (and rewrite!) routines that handle low-level tasks that many processes have in common. That is why so much software today—including application servers—rely on object-oriented programming and components.

This notion of reusing code is explored further in the next chapter. Is it necessary to customize your code for each database that you might use? (The answer, of course, is no.)

Connecting to
Data: ODBC
and JDBC

8

The application server architecture features the ability to replace interface, database, and application server as circumstances change. The idea of a structured environment with common interfaces is not new. One of the prime examples of such an environment is the world of databases. Originally, each database product came with its own interface and programming environment: if you changed the database, you had to change the interface (and vice versa).

The development and adoption of SQL was one way to standardize programming interfaces to databases. However, embedded SQL—the SQL commands you placed in your program—still needed to be tweaked and fiddled with if you changed databases.

As you will see in this chapter, there are now a variety of tools that you can use to access a generic database from a program; you can then change that database at will. The trend is a continuing abstraction of data away from the reality of the specific database and its storage mechanism.

ODBC

Open Database Connectivity (ODBC) was developed by Microsoft in 1991. Based on the X/Open Call-Level Interface, it addressed the need to be able to write programs that could communicate with databases without knowing the specific database system's interface needs.

ODBC Components

In order to formalize the interface between application and database, ODBC describes four main components:

1. applications,

2. databases,

3. database drivers, and

4. driver managers.

Applications and databases have their traditional meanings. Database drivers are libraries of code that perform the actual interaction with a database. A database driver needs to be available for the specific database that you are using—Oracle, SQL Server, DB2, and so forth.

A driver manager is the library of code with which an application program interacts. At run time, the driver manager establishes a connection to the appropriate database driver(s) to carry out your commands. The driver manager is not specific to individual databases—a single driver manager can interact with database drivers for Oracle, SQL Server, DB2, and so forth.

Types of Database Drivers

There are three basic types of database drivers:

1. one-tier drivers,

2. two-tier drivers, and

3. three-tier drivers.

One-Tier Drivers

One-tier drivers access flat files (such as ISAM files or Excel spreadsheets). They can map the incoming SQL commands from the application program and driver manager to the appropriate commands for the flat files.

Two-Tier Drivers

Two-tier drivers access SQL-compliant databases directly. Instead of reprocessing SQL commands to the format of a flat file, they pass the SQL on to the database. They are called two-tier drivers because conceptually they have both client (application) and server (database) tiers. The two tiers can be on two computers or on a single computer. Two-tier refers to the architecture, not the hardware configuration.

Three-Tier Drivers

A three-tier driver differs from a two-tier driver in that the driver manager and database driver are on a computer separate from both the application program and the database. Three-tier drivers thus use communication links for their communications both with the application program and with the database. Three computers are typically involved: a client, a gateway server (for the driver manager and database driver), and a database server.

Where Drivers Come From

A database driver needs to be able to interact with the database and run either on the same computer with the database or on a computer that can communicate with the database. Database drives are often provided by database vendors, but they also are often provided by third parties.

If a database's API is published (and most of them are), it is not particularly difficult to write a database driver for that database. There are companies (Intersolv is one) that specialize in writing database drivers for a variety of databases on a variety of platforms.

Transactions and Concurrency

As with any software that mediates between components, ODBC has the ability to be more than just a message-relayer. In the case of ODBC, it is important to note that transaction management and concurrency control can be managed at the ODBC layer.

Transaction management and concurrency control can also be managed at the database level and at the application server level. In most cases, you will not have a problem finding one of your software components to handle these tasks: your problem will be choosing which already-installed software to use.

JDBC

Like ODBC, Java Database Connectivity (JDBC) provides a database-independent way of writing code (in this case Java code). You can use JDBC with any SQL database, and you can even use it on top of ODBC.

JDBC has the same four components as ODBC, and they serve the same purposes. By comparison with ODBC, JDBC provides the features of Java which include a high degree of network awareness, very rigorous security, and the object-oriented nature of Java.

Both ODBC and JDBC provide a dramatically simplified way of dealing with a variety of database products when compared to the older method of writing directly to a specific database API. Their logical simplicity sometimes belies the complexity of their implementations. However, the point of this architecture is that those implementations are hidden from users and system implementors and integrators.

OLE DB

OLE DB is Microsoft's set of ActiveX interfaces that can access data. It is not limited to databases or SQL-type data. OLE DB replaces the traditional driver manager in the ODBC architecture; it is a component that is called from the application program, and it interacts directly with database (and other) drivers.

Since OLE DB provides an object-oriented interface, it is usable in the world of COM components described in the previous chapter. It is a broader and more modern implementation of ODBC (which it subsumes in many ways).

ActiveX Data Objects (ADO)

ActiveX Data Objects can access OLE DB and can be used from Java or Visual Basic. They further the process of abstracting data sources, since an application program can talk to an ADO which in turn talks to OLE DB and thence to databases.

Note that OLE DB is a set of ActiveX interfaces; ADO are actually objects.

What This Means for Application Servers

The continuing abstraction of databases generally means that you are less tied to a specific product. When you attempt to put the pieces of the puzzle together, you do not need to find an application server that communicates with your legacy database system: you need only make certain that both the application server and the legacy database system both support ODBC, JDBC, or OLE DB.

Some application servers (particularly those developed by database manufacturers) provide direct interaction between the application server and the database's API. This can be very efficient—and can help you reuse much legacy code that already uses that API.

However, using these intermediaries such as ODBC and JDBC can position you well for the future: if you change databases—or if the database's API changes—it is often easier to handle such changes with ODBC and JDBC. Furthermore, from a management point of view, it is often easier to find ODBC/JDBC programmers than experts in a particular database technology.

Summary

Through the evolution of these architectures, more and more code is moved into the middle layers—out of the databases and application programs. There is much commonality in the requirements for this code, and while early programs did implement their own transaction management and locking, that is handled today by the products mentioned in this chapter.

This part of the book has provided an overview of the technologies involved in implementation of systems based on application servers. One overarching theme is clear: this is a world of components and objects. That world is, by definition, a world of interoperability, although some vendors are more interoperable than others.

A long tradition in the computer industry has the industry leaders frowning on interoperability and the other players endorsing it. The leader—be it IBM, Microsoft, or Remington Rand—proposes that uniform standards and single-vendor sourcing provide the greatest benefits. The others suggest that flexibility and interoperability are in the users' best interest.

The computer world is moving from its first half century—a century of custom-designed and hand-crafted artifacts to a world of mass production and interchangeable parts. (Eli Whitney would be proud!)

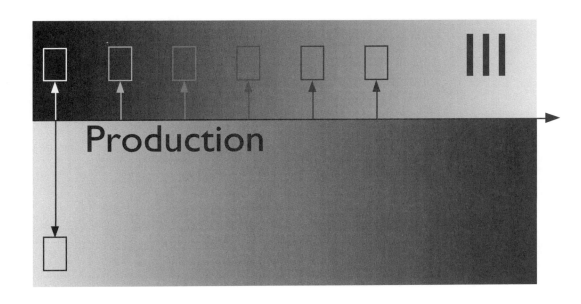

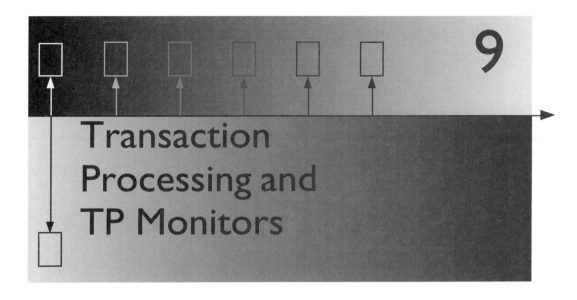

Transaction Processing and TP Monitors

9

Application servers frequently are used to manage transactions. These are the frequently complex interactions between user and system that go beyond a single mouse click. They are complex in all cases, and on the Web they are particularly daunting. This is not only because Web connections are inherently unstable (the protocols are designed to continue to function even with serious telecommunications failures and the vast distances and complexity of connections are continuing sources of difficulty), but also because the Web's HTTP protocol is stateless—and preservation of state is a critical aspect of transaction processing.

This chapter provides you with a basic definition and overview of transaction processing. Thereafter, you will find information on:

- *Transaction standards, including OMG's Object Transaction Service, Java Transaction, X/Open XA and TX, and Oracle Transaction Service.*

- *Small-scale transaction monitors. (If you think all this is over your head or far too complex for your operations, this section is for you.)*

Transaction Processing: An Overview

Application servers frequently are used to support transaction processing operations. These operations have been at the heart of many online computer systems. There are two primary ways of looking at transactions, as the following description shows (italics added):

> The term transaction is often applied to a wide variety of business and computer functions. Looked at as a computer function, a transaction could refer to a *set of operations* including disk read/writes, operating system calls, or some form of data transfer from one subsystem to another.

> ... the TPC regards a transaction as it is commonly understood in the business world: *a commercial exchange of goods, services, or money.* A typical transaction, as defined by the TPC, would include the updating to a database system for such things as inventory control (goods), airline reservations (services), or banking (money).[1]

---

1. The TPC [Transaction Processing Performance Council] is a non-profit corporation founded to define transaction processing and database benchmarks and to disseminate objective, verifiable TPC performance data to the industry. Their Web page, from which this text is taken, is at http://www.tpc.org/missionandscope.html

Transactions Are a Unified Operation	A transaction is a set of operations that are handled as a single unit. From the computer system's point of view, that is all that a transaction is; its purpose is immaterial, but its unity is critical.
Transactions Are Commercial	As the second paragraph states, the common understanding of a transaction is of a commercial operation—an exchange of goods, services, or money. Here is where the transactional nature of the process comes into play: two (or more) operations must be treated as a single entity. For example, the payment of money for a real estate transaction is part and parcel of the change in ownership listed on the deed. Neither part of the transaction should be processed on its own. The commercial nature of transactions is also important to note. Value is exchanged on both sides of the transaction; as a result, the stakes involved in losing all or part of a transaction can be higher than when an e-mail message goes astray.
Transactions Versus Analysis	Online Transaction Processing (OLTP) is often constrasted with Online Analytical Processing (OLAP). To some people, there is a clear distinction between OLTP, which processes sets of operations as single entities (often with value changing hands), and OLAP, which is a technology that provides relational database data in a variety of formats and views to people who are searching for trends either manually or with automated tools. In fact, the boundary between analysis and transaction is often blurred in real life. The transition from "just looking" to "I'll take this" is the essence of modern retailing, and insistence on a clearcut line of demarcation in the technology sector is inconsistent with this trend.

Do You Use Transactions?	If your operation involves transactions, your entire environment including application server and databases must be able to support transactions. Furthermore, you must write your custom-written code with transactions in mind.
	There is significant overhead to transactions, both on the processing side and on the development and maintenance side. It may turn out that you do not have transactions in the traditional sense of the word. If the operations that you carry out with your customers involve significant manual processing, the actual transaction—the exchange of goods, money, and services—may not need to be supported in your software. A company that sells electronic books online must be able to handle transactions in its customer support system; a company that hangs wallpaper need not necessarily handle transactions since the primary processing (the wallpaper hanging) does not involve the computer system.
Terminology	Transaction processing (TP for short) has its own set of terminology. The key term, of course, is transaction—the unit of work. Four properties of transactions are commonly discussed; they make up the acronym ACID.
Atomicity	This is the notion that a transaction cannot happen partially: either all of the operations or none of them occur.
Consistency	The database that is at the core of a transaction processing system remains consistent across transactions. In other words, a transaction cannot corrupt the database.
Isolation	Isolated (serializable) transactions appear to be executed sequentially, that is, one after the other. Although parts of transactions may occur in an interleaved fashion, the atomic transaction occurs at a single moment in time—and that is a moment before or after all other transactions being processed.

Durability

Once a transaction is completed, it remains completed despite possible problems elsewhere in the system. The terms persistent and stable are often used in place of durability.

Other terminology used in TP has been described previously in this book. In particular, TP involves client/server systems, with the server typically containing or being connected to one or more databases.

TP also implies distributed processing—the extension of client/server to clusters of computers, mirrored sites, replicated databases, and so forth. If all of the processing occurs on a single computer, the issues involved in TP become rather simple.

Types of Transactions

There are three types of transactions that are normally recognized:

1. flat transactions,

2. nested transactions, and

3. chained transactions.

Flat Transactions

Flat transactions are the most basic transactions. At the start of a transaction, the resources necessary for its completion are obtained and locked to prevent them from being updated by others. On completion, database changes are committed and resources are released.

Nested Transactions

Most transaction processing systems allow for nesting of transactions—subtransactions that are processed within a larger one. Each nested transaction can be completed and committed while the global transaction is still in progress. If the global transaction fails, all of the nested transactions are rolled back.

Chained Transactions

Another type of transaction involves subtransactions that can be committed independently of the global transaction. In a chained transaction, subtransactions commit (irrevocably), but the resources needed for the entire transaction remain locked until everything is completed.

Who Is Responsible for Transaction Processing?

Transaction processing is made possible by the collection of a variety of individual steps into a single process with the ACID properties listed previously. This can be done either by the database or by the application server. Modern high-end databases such as Oracle, DB2, Informix, and Sybase all support transactions at the database level. It can also be done by the application server; in that case, the application server is responsible for collecting the individual steps and either applying them together or undoing them together.

It is quite possible to work with both a database and application server, each of which can create and manage transactions. In such cases, you need to decide which product will be primary. If your processing involves a database that interacts not only with your application server but also with a variety of legacy applications, it may be important to let the database handle transactions.

On the other hand, remember that your database may be the bottleneck of your operation. High-end application servers can be deployed on a number of computers and manage their interactions as if they were on a single computer. In such cases, it may be better to let the application server handle transactions since more computing power is available to it.

Operational Issues

Three operational issues in particular are of importance to TP, and if you need to support transactions, your application server and/or database must deal with these issues. They are fault tolerance, concurrency and locks, and recovery. All of these apply to transactions being processed both by databases and by application servers; any of them (or all) may be implemented on databases as well as on application servers.

Fault Tolerance

A well-designed TP system must be able to accomodate failures at any point in the system. With Internet-based systems, the failure is commonly in the communications network, but anything else can fail. If you are coming from the desktop environment, you may be used to rebooting your computer. As old-time mainframers will tell you, the notion of rebooting an online transaction processing system is scandalous. You do not reboot a system to which several thousand people are connected. (If you do, you are likely to make the front page of the papers.)

Fault tolerance is something that needs to be built into your system at every stage of the process. From your data entry Web pages to database structures, constantly ask yourself, "What if this doesn't happen?" If the answer is, "Start over," then that's what you should do—it is easier for you to start over than for the potential customer to start over (with another vendor).

Fault tolerance is designed into the operations of your database and application server; however, you are responsible for designing it and implementing it in the code that you write and the Web pages you design.

Concurrency and Locks

The heart of transaction processing is concurrency and locks—the ability of multiple users to access a database and other resources as if they were the only users in the system. Databases and application servers that support transaction processing implement concurrency and locks.

You are responsible for using those features, but you should not have to program any concurrency or locks for your applications. If you find yourself developing such software (for example, implementing "in use" flags or semaphores), go back to your documentation. You should find these features there and you are better off using the standard tools than reimplementing these items on your own.

If you do not find such features in your application server or database, you need to find products that do support concurrency and locks.

Most databases and application servers support concurrency and locks at a reasonably sophisticated level. If your demands are likely to be more extreme—as in the case of a system with many simultaneous users—focus on those features in choosing your application server.

Recovery

Finally, it is not enough that an application server and a database should be capable of recovering from problems. Fault tolerance refers to the ability of the system to continue functioning properly even in the face of adversity; recovery refers to the ability of the system to restore itself to normal processing after a failure.

Recovery has many faces. Do not look at it simply from the point of view of your application server and your database. Part of recovery involves the operational staff. Today's online systems are expected to work 24 hours a day, 7 days a week.

TP Monitors

Transaction processing monitors (TP monitors, for short) are programs that help to implement transaction processing. The interactions described so far in this book have been for the most part between two entities: a user's Web browser and a Web server; between the Web server and plug-ins, helpers, or other applications; or between database management systems and application servers or other middleware products.

In the real world—particularly the world of large-scale systems—there may be multiple instances of these entities. A Web site can be mirrored on a number of different physical servers. Likewise, a database can be mirrored on a number of different computers so that its load can be served appropriately.

A TP monitor can be seen as implementing the interaction between these entities—between an application server, for example, and the database on which it relies. The TP monitor can move messages between the particular Web server that handles a user's request and the particular mirrored database that contains the data. (Note that this scenario envisions copies of the Web server and copies of the database: they are to all intents and purposes identical. TP monitors are not normally involved in the alternate routing of transactions to different types of databases or Web sites.)

The TP monitor not only can ensure that transactions are handled as simply as they would be if a single two-way relationship between application server and database or Web server existed, their handling of transactions can determine which resource (database, Web server, and so forth) is used. Thus, load balancing for large systems can be achieved.

TP monitors are normally used in large-scale systems; transaction processing and its concepts apply to large- and small-scale systems that handle transactions.

Transaction Processing Standards and Architectures

Transaction processing standards have been devised to help not only in the development of transaction processing systems but also to aid in product-by-product comparisons and benchmarks. Some of the important standards are described in this section:

- X/Open XA and TX
- CORBA Object Transaction Service
- Java Transaction Service
- Oracle Transaction Service

X/Open XA and TX

The Open Group (X/Open), has defined a Distributed Transaction Processing (DTP) Model which is widely implemented. Devised in the early 1990s, it addressed the issue of how to combine software elements from a variety of vendors in a way that would allow transactions to be handled properly.

The DTP Model

The DTP model defines three elements:

1. A resource manager controls a resource such as a database (the use of the term "resource" allows a more general view than just that of databases).

2. An application program implements business logic and accesses the resource manager's resources.

3. A transaction manager is used to manage the transactions.

Standards and protocols for communications between pairs of these elements are:

- SQL for communication between applications and resource managers.

- The X/Open TX (transaction demarcation) specification for communication between application programs and transaction managers. (The XATMI specification provides a variation for the client/server model.)

- The X/Open XA specification for communication between transaction manager and resource managers.

From the standpoint of implementers, the X/Open DTP specification consists of the X/Open TX and X/Open XA interfaces.

What It Means for Application Servers

Many application servers fit into this model in one way or another. Some application servers encompass all three parts of the DTP model, providing resource manager (for their own database), transaction manager, and the application in the form of your servlets and other code for the application server.

Other application servers merely consist of one or two of the DTP model components: you provide the others. The importance of adherence to the DTP model is that if you need to mix and match components, you can do so from the wide variety of components that are based on the X/Open model.

CORBA Object Transaction Service

The CORBA Object Transaction Service (OTS) is interoperable with the X/Open DTP model. There is a one-to-one mapping for many elements of the TX and XA interfaces.

The OTS Model

The Object Transaction Service is object-oriented. Thus, you will find that tx_begin() maps to Current::begin(), xa_prepare() maps to Resource::prepare, and so forth.

The mapping is not complete: a few TX and XA calls have no equivalents in OTS and vice versa. Nevertheless, the design of OTS was created to build on and to interoperate with TX and XA both for architectural and commercial purposes.

Because OTS is built on CORBA, it is able to use CORBA's specifications for the Internet InterORB Protocol (IIOP) to implement the distributed aspects of its transaction processing.

What This Means for Application Servers

Because of the interoperability, you can consider OTS and X/Open DTP as very close partners. Replacing a component from one architecture with one from the other is not a transparent operation, but it is relatively simple.

Java Transaction Service

Java Transaction Service (JTS) builds on OTS in a Java-based, object-oriented environment. It takes the three-element DTP model and adds to it. Not surprisingly, those additions make the use of Java even easier.

The JTS Model

In the JTS Model, the transaction manager mediates among three players:

1. the resource manager,

2. the application server, and

3. the application.

(Compare this to the DTP model in which the application server and application are a single element.)

In addition, the communications resource manager (a part of the XATMI client/server model) is made explicit.

Two-way communications between these components are based largely on Java APIs. In particular:

- The application and application server interact using Enterprise Java Beans.

- Interaction between the application server and the resource manager is via JDBC or JMS.

- Communications between either the application, application server, or resource manager are via the javax.transaction class.

- Communications to and from the Communication Resource Manager are via IIOP.

What This Means for Application Servers

The progression here—from X/Open DTP to OTS and then to JTS—is both historical and logical. Each step is more object-oriented and provides a simpler interface with less code to be written. However, since all three of the models are basically interoperable, you should be able to mix and match elements relatively easily.

The most important point to remember, however, is that this is the basic model of transaction processing that is implemented today for many, many systems.

Microsoft Transaction Server

The Microsoft Transaction Server (MTS) provides a model that is at the same time similar to and different from these. As with most Microsoft technologies, MTS is embedded deeply in Windows. This makes it hard (if not impossible) to use MTS technology on other platforms; furthermore, the modularization and replaceability of the elements of DTP is not nearly so present in MTS.

This is not meant as a criticism of MTS, it is just a statement of where MTS is at the moment. Whether it evolves into a more open or more closed architecture depends on a variety of factors including the market environment, among others.

Small Scale Transaction Monitors

Transaction processing can be implemented in very small scale application servers: you will find transaction support in Tango and Cold Fusion, for example. Transaction processing is not just about high-volume e-commerce Web sites, it is also part of standard programming practice.

For example, if you use a basic accounting program, you may decide to write a check to someone you have never dealt with before. As a result of this decision, you may enter a new payee (with address and other information) and then the check. If you cancel the operation—exactly what is cancelled? The check? The check and the payee information? Do you have a choice?

In fact, human beings normally think in terms of transactions; it is programmers who break them up into (supposedly) logical components. The most basic operations—such as going to the store to buy dog food—consist of many steps.

Transaction processing can be built into databases or application servers (or both). You can also create your own—and many programmers have done so. You will find the germs of transaction processing in flags and semaphors marked "In progress," "Pending," or "Complete." If your experience is not in traditional IT, you may be tempted to do such things yourself. Be careful. If you need to use transactions, make certain that your application server (or database) supports them.

If your application server does not support transactions, you will almost always be better off upgrading to one that does rather than trying to get around the limitation. Your first step, however, should be to contact your vendor: almost every application server (even the smallest) supports transactions either now or in the immediate future.

Summary

As soon as you get beyond the simplest request to display a static Web page, you tend to get into the world of transactions. This is a world in which a series of logically connected user actions must be assembled into one transaction that consummates an e-commerce sale, develops a complex query, or otherwise interacts with servers and databases.

Since HTTP is a stateless protocol, transactions need to be implemented either in the application server or in the database—or in both of them. Special-purpose applications called TP monitors may be used to implement transactions; they also are used to support duplicated and mirrored databases and servers. While transaction processing can affect the smallest dynamic Web site, the use of TP monitors for load balancing in this way is normally confined to larger sites.

As noted in the definition of transactions at the beginning of this chapter, they are very often commercial in nature, involving the exchange of money and other items of value (goods or information). As soon as you are dealing with such items, the issue of security arises. It is discussed in the next chapter.

Security and Application Servers

Application servers routinely deal with information that needs to be handled carefully. E-commerce—like traditional commerce—involves the exchange of money for goods or services. Just as people use safes and armored cars, locks on their doors, and other reasonable precautions to protect their valuables, so, too, security applies to computer systems.

Many application servers (particularly the larger ones aimed at the enterprise markets) incorporate sophisticated security mechanisms. Others rely on the security mechanisms of the computers on which they reside. Regardless of what type of application server you are using, you need to be aware not only of the security issues that can be involved but of the ways in which you can address them.

This chapter provides a brief overview to help you determine the type of security issues that you need to consider; it then covers the security options available at different parts of Internet-based systems in general, the issue of authentication, directories of information, and security concerns in your overall operation.

Do You Need Security?

Not every Web site needs security, but most do. Security applies to all aspects of your Web site, from the pages themselves to the transactions that may be processed while most people are sleeping.

Securing the Site

When you open a Web site to the public, you are inviting people to use their computers to access your information. Despite basic precautions you can take, the site is often vulnerable to significant unintended exposure. This comes from three areas: sightseers, borrowers, and hackers.

Sightseers

Most browsers allow you to view the source code of the Web pages that you visit. HTML is, after all, text-based, and it is not hard to view the source and make sense of it. You should assume that people will do this (it happens to be a very good way to learn how to construct Web sites).

Since your raw HTML is visible in this way, be careful about what it contains. Comments may not be visible on your Web site, but they are visible in this way. Telephone numbers and even passwords are often discovered.

In general, sightseers do not pose much of a problem. They are just looking around.

Borrowers

Borrowers pose more of a risk. Since it is so easy to view HTML source code, many people look at the source code for a Web feature that they particularly like and then "borrow" it. Source code for many simple Web operations tends to propagate across the Web rather quickly.

Your exposure comes if you have used proprietary code on your page. If someone "borrows" code that you wrote, that is one thing; however, if you allow someone to borrow copyrighted code that you do not have the right to distribute, you can be exposed to problems. You can achieve a certain degree of security with such code by placing it inside scripts or servlets that themselves are not visible to the public. In any event, make certain that your source code contains a satisfactory copyright notice and warning about reuse.

Hackers

The biggest concern you have is hackers: people who for malicious purposes want to disrupt your Web site. Many hackers are sightseers with attitude: they start by just looking around, but can't resist the temptation to exploit a problem they see or otherwise cause nuisance.

What to Do

There are many books dealing with security on Web sites: make certain that you read enough of them to scare yourself into taking action. Here are the denials that you must not allow yourself to cling to:

- No one would care about our site—it is too obscure.

- Everyone who works here is trustworthy.

- There are no links to this page—no one will ever get to it.

Deal with the password issue before it becomes a problem. The issue is that there are simply too many passwords being used today; most people suffer from password-overload, and they violate the most basic security concerns. Here are some standard precautions with regard to passwords: few people abide by all of them.

- Change your password routinely.

- Do not write the password down.

- Do not use the same password twice.

- Do not store the password in software (as in automated log-on scripts) unless the computer on which the software resides is itself passworded or kept under lock and key.

If you have to make compromises with these basic standards, make them in a systematic way, rather than on an ad hoc basis.

Securing the Operations and Transactions

The security issues outlined in the previous section apply to all Web sites. Application servers frequently support e-commerce transactions, and a separate and more complicated set of security considerations needs to be applied to those operations. Since they go on (in most cases) 24 hours a day, and since they frequently occur with minimal if any human oversight, you need to set up precautions to ensure that the transactions are successful and that neither you nor your customers are defrauded.

Security over TCP/IP

TCP/IP is the communications architecture that is used for the Internet. It is designed in a layered approach, with seven layers. Each layer provides a different type of operation. TCP/IP is implemented in a wide range of devices, and this clear standard makes it possible for them to communicate.

The seven layers of TCP/IP adhere to two primary rules:

1. A layer can communicate with the layers immediately above and below it, but cannot communicate with layers further away. This makes for very structured and modularized code in the implementation.

2. A layer at one end of a connection communicates directly with its peer at the other end of a connection. It cannot communicate with any other part of the connection at the other end.

Security can be implemented in a number of the TCP/IP layers; each layer poses different security risks and different options.

Physical Layer

The physical layer consists of cabling and connectors.

Why to Implement Security

The primary reason for implementing security at the physical layer is to prevent damage to your network. Eavesdropping and wiretapping are certainly issues in many areas, but it is inefficient to divert information at the physical layer—you have to figure out what those bits and bytes represent.

The integrity of the network, however, is another matter. Periodically you read of critical networks (such as air traffic control) being brought down by accidents with construction equipment. Securing your network can minimize such problems.

How to Implement Security

Security at this layer can be implemented very simply—and securely. Lock the door to the room in which devices are stored; run cables through secure spaces. This is the oldest and strongest form of security. Of course, if you are using the public telecommunications network, you do not control the physical layer, and this is not possible. Note, however, that many truly confidential networks—such as those used for defense—do not use the public network just for this reason.)

Securing the network involves not just keeping unauthorized people out but also keeping cabling properly bundled and off the floor.

Data Link Layer

This layer involves the operations involved in moving data across the network. Ethernet is primarily a data link layer technology; other aspects of the data link layer include network topology, error notification, sequencing of frames, and flow control.

Network Layer

The network layer handles communications around the network; IP logical addressing and routing protocols are often part of this layer.

Why to Implement Security

Although this part of the network may not be under your control, you should pay attention to the routing tables that are used for your Web site. If someone gains access to the Internet directories that convert IP addresses to domain names and vice versa, they can send traffic astray. This has happened on several occasions. Most frequently, problems here are a result of carelessness and error.

How to Implement Security

Updates to your network's routing tables need to be made in a systematic way. Adding devices to a local area network can be simple, but can also cause problems. Resist the temptation to bypass the procedures that you should have in place. Updating the tables may seem to be a trivial and clerical task, but it should be done by two people (one to make the change and the other to review it).

As with backing up your hard disk, this is something that most people do only after they have been through an unnecessary disaster.

Transport Layer

The transport layer deals with packetizing of information: it takes a data stream coming to or from an application program and breaks it into the individual packets of data that are sent over the network (which is often referred to as a packet-switching network).

Security implemented at the transport layer automatically makes communications of all sorts secure. The application layer of TCP/IP (the topmost layer) supports protocols such as FTP, HTTP, and NNTP (news). Thus, each of those protocols can be made secure if it uses a secure transport layer.

How to Implement Security

The Secure Socket Layer (SSL) technology is used to encrypt messages at this layer. The encryption involves the use of keys—128-bit keys are now standard. (The longer the key, the more difficult it is to decipher the encrypted message.)

SSL provides three types of security support:

1. Server authentication: this lets the client (user) know that communications are with the server that the client expects.

2. Client authentication: this is the reverse of the previous type of security, and it lets the server know that the client is who it claims to be.

3. Encryption: messages are coded as they are transmitted.

Because SSL involves additional processing and transmission of messages, it is slower than standard communications.

Therefore, you should only use it for messages that in fact need encryption, such as a form that a user submits with credit card or other information.

Why to Implement Security

Encrypting communications—such as credit card numbers—often gives a false sense of security. Far more damage is done by people strolling past a computer and glancing at the screen than by electronically intercepting communications. However, your implementation of security at this level may be required either by your organization's policies or by your customers' expectations.

Session Layer

This part of the protocol deals with remote procedure calls—requesting that programs be run on a distant computer. COM and CORBA both rely heavily on remote procedure calls. Security for this layer is usually implemented through applications and protocols, not directly through TCP/IP.

Presentation Layer

The presentation layer consists of the standards and protocols that govern the display of data. Such standards as GIF, Quick-Time, MPEG, JPEG, and TIFF are part of the presentation layer.

Application Layer

The application layer represents the protocols that you are familiar with: protocols such as HTTP, FTP, Telnet, and SMTP. Any of these protocols can be enhanced with security.

Note that implementations of security at lower levels of TCP/IP are available to all protocols. Thus, SSL (implemented at the transport level) automatically makes all of the application layer protocols secure with regard to the issues that it protects.

How to
Implement
Security

The Secure HyperText Transfer Protocol (S-HTTP) is designed for use in conjunction with HTTP. Like SSL, S-HTTP needs to be implemented on your Web server and supported on your user's browser.

Why to
Implement
Security

Implementing security at the application layer can be appropriate for extending basic security such as SSL as well as for cases in which you can control the application layer (via the application server or Web server) but not the transport layer.

X.509 Certificates

As part of the authentication procedures used in SSL and other security mechanisms, the concept of a trusted third party often comes into play. This is demonstrated in the use of certificates—a means of certifying that data is from its purported source.

The most widely used certificate standard is promulgated by the International Telecommunication Union (ITU-T), formerly known as CCITT. The protocol, known as X.509, provides for a certificate with a variety of standard data including the subject or user name, version and validity information, and various identifiers. When a certificate is processed, the software that is attempting to verify it looks at the identity of the certificate authority (CA)—the issuer of the certificate. If the software recognizes that CA as one that it trusts, it accepts the certificate. If it does not trust the CA, it gets the CA's certificate and looks at its issuer. If it trusts the CA's CA, all is well; if not, the process continues until either a trusted third party is found or the search fails.

Note that in this architecture, the trusted third party that actually is used can vary from computer to computer depending on which CAs that particular computer has encountered and trusted.

Certificates can be supported on Web servers, in application servers, or as part of lower-level security and cryptographic processes. They are needed for a great many security operations; their presence in an application server is not a major differentiation among products, since they are so widely used. (However, this does not stop companies from marketing them as if they were the latest thing since sliced bread.)

Access and Directories

Access Control Lists (ACLs) and Lightweight Directory Access Protocol (LDAP) are among the products and standards that are used to control access and manage networks and their users. Lightweight application servers use the directory services of the systems on which they run; larger application servers may implement their own access control and directory services.

You can very easily find yourself with a multitude of directories and access control mechanisms: one for your database(s), one for your Web server, one for your application server, one for your network (such as Novell's Directory Service—NDS), and so forth. Keeping them synchronized is one of the reasons for using a common protocol such as LDAP.

However, this approach (which is widely promoted) often is impractical in the real world. Try this test: go through your entire system (database, applets, servlets, server environment tables, and so forth) looking for directories and access controls. You will probably find them in a number of places.

For example, the database may have a customer or vendor database: it may have access information used in deciding whether or not a particular user can access certain data. Such a user may come into your system over the Internet as a public (i.e., unidentified) user: you manipulate access and security based on the database fields, not on the access control list.

You may find conflicting access controls and duplicate directories (it would be surprising if you did not). The danger here is that in maintaining access controls and directories, you maintain the wrong ones. A vast number of people who have put up interactive Web sites with any kind of security have found themselves manipulating the wrong directories.

Before this happens, make certain that you know what is stored where and what tables and access controls need to be manipulated. Centralizing all directory information is a great goal, but the more achievable goal of knowing where you have put everything is often more valuable.

Security at the User's End

You have a certain responsibility for security at the user's end of the connection. If you are running an e-commerce site, and you ask your customers to use a password, remember that you may be causing them to write down the password and tape it to their monitor—a common result of password surfeit. People frequently use the same password over and over (although this is very much not recommended). You may come into possession of someone's banking identification number—just because it is the same as the password chosen for your site.

If you are dealing with the public at large, consider adding a paragraph about passwords and security to your site's basic information. If you are dealing with a private system—such as an organization's Human Resources Web site, your responsibility may be greater, and your clout more effective. Remember that you are bringing up the security issue in asking people to use a password; deal with it completely by reminding people how to use passwords properly.

Security in Operations

The types of security available to you are comparable to those available only to financial institutions and other such entities a few years ago. The fact that anyone can set up a Web site with secure information on it is remarkable. Remember, though, that all is for naught if passwords are taped to walls, access control lists are not updated, and other basic precautions are not taken. If your Web site has security on it, make certain that your work environment is equally secure.

Summary

Security is not something that you can add on to a project at the end. This chapter has covered the major issues of security that you should consider when developing a project using application servers (and Web sites in general).

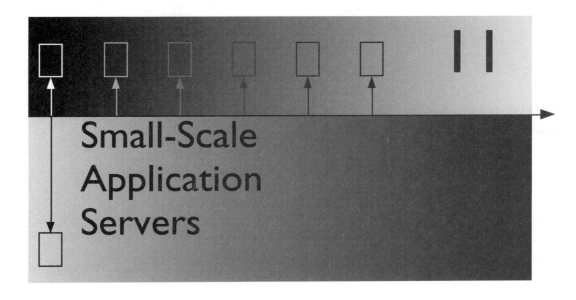

Small-Scale Application Servers

Small scale application servers—those based on HTML or provided as part of personal-computer database products—have an important role to play. Remember that application servers are as much an architecture and design model as a product category. The design that you apply to small-scale application servers can be used with large-scale application servers.

This chapter provides some tips for working with small-scale application servers. Specifically, it covers

- *using small-scale application servers as a training tool,*

- *prototyping with small-scale application servers, and*

- *scalability issues.*

Small-Scale Application Servers as Training Tools

Small-scale application servers are an invaluable training tool, particularly if you are new to this type of environment. By yourself—and using only your personal computer—you can set up a full-fledged application server environment to which you can connect over an intranet, the Internet, or just on your own computer. (You will probably need an IP address for your computer: see *Database-Driven Web Sites* for more details.)

Using the diagrams presented in the first part of this book, identify them in your application server. (In small-scale servers, several features may be bundled together—as, for example, transaction processing and a database.) Design a test case using the application server architecture described here. Be punctilious about not using shortcuts and bypasses that may be available only in your application server.

Use the Examples	Every application server product large and small ships with samples. No matter how boring it is, install, run, and test a sample. This will expose problems in installation and configuration. It is remarkable how many people skip this step, but if you do, you will most likely lose time—a lot of it—later.
Learn How to Test	Do not just test that things work: test that things fail properly when accidents happen. Try unplugging communications cables to find out what happens (mark them first so that you can reconnect them!). Keep track of your testing. Remember that when you place your application server-based system on the Internet (or even on an intranet), a very large number of people will be using it and judging you and your organization by its results.

Create a
Usability Lab

The user is king on the Internet. In the old days of mainframe computers and the early personal computers, many people were intimidated by computers. Today, however, people of all ages are using complex software to surf the Net and send e-mail messages around the world. This is empowering them—and empowering them to ask, "Why can I send a message to the Yukon but I can't make this query work?" The further empowerment is that now that they can send their e-mail messages to the Yukon, they are starting to blame the software—not themselves—when things do not work properly.

Usability testing is a key to developing an effective Web site. You can create a sophisticated usability lab with a one-way mirror to observe people using the site. You can create a more modest lab by asking someone to use your site and by observing them.

Watch for Errors

It is tempting to watch how people successfully navigate your site and use the dynamic pages that are powered by your database and application server. If you are in the same room with them, they may congratulate you or express thanks.

This is not at all useful.

Watch (silently!) for errors. Do not respond to questions—after all, your users will be alone at their computers. (Be very careful: many people tend to make little noises or gestures as they see the mouse being moved in the wrong direction or a word being misspelled.)

Remember that the errors you spot visually are those that your code is likely to catch (after all, they are what you perceive as errors). Did you ever think that anyone would enter "Help" for their name? Some people type "Help" anywhere they can in the assumption that a pop-up window will materialize with information. Let the page fail; if it crashes or no error message materializes, just write it down.

Do not take it personally. It may be your baby, but your skill is in devising the design or implementation; if you insist on being perfect, this business is not for you. Do the best you can, observe, and learn from mistakes (preferably those of others).

Keep Your Hands Off the Keyboard   It is incredibly tempting to give cues—either physical or verbal. You may also see that someone is heading into an area that is not part of your test, and so it makes sense to take over "for a few moments" until that side trip is navigated. Do not do this. Remember your ultimate user, alone at a terminal. Let things break (and then go back and prevent it from happening).

Prototyping with Small-Scale Application Servers

Another valuable use of small-scale application servers is to prototype systems that you want to build. Particularly in an enterprise IT environment, it is not always easy to bring up a test database and a test Web site. By focusing on the underlying architecture of application servers, you can do this with a desktop database such as FileMaker Pro or with an application server such as Cold Fusion or Tango.

Preparing to Scale

Scalability is a feature of many application servers, but scalability from small-scale application servers to larger ones is sometimes problematic. Use the general architecture of application servers and eschew unique features of the product you are dealing with. In that way, you will be able to scale your system most easily.

Note that scalability almost always refers to enlarging a system's scope. Enterprises grow, e-commerce sites expand, and more and more people need to use your site. As a result, you may find that once you have scaled up you can afford to use product-specific features.

However, do not ignore the fact that you may need to downscale your application at some point. As applications grow, one way of handling their growth is by splitting them. A company such as amazon.com grows by adding products such as music and toys to their initial offerings of books. Other companies handle growth by splitting or reorgnizing their products and divisional structure. Making certain that your system can scale in either direction will make it more robust.

The Moral

The theme of this chapter (and of good software design in general) is to make as few assumptions as possible and to document them as well as you can. If you assume that all of your users will know what "4t0" means, make certain that is clear. Many system problems—and probably most interface problems—rest on faulty assumptions.

Summary

This part of the book has covered issues that affect the largest application server-based systems such as TP monitors as well as issues that affect large and small systems such as transaction management and security.

What if you want to test a concept, develop a prototype, or just learn how to use application servers? In this chapter, the roles of small-scale application servers have been discussed. They can help you achieve those ends.

The first part of this book provided you with the basics of the technologies that underpin application servers. In the second part, you saw the details of those technologies and how they can be used with application servers. This part has addressed specific issues of implementation. All that is left is thinking about how to maintain application server systems once you have developed them and put them into production. That is the topic of the final part of this book.

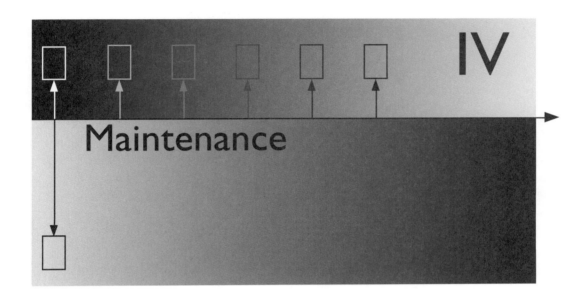

Designing for Maintenance

Web sites are notoriously hard to maintain, in part because they change so frequently. Dynamic Web sites are even more difficult, since the pages that users see can be created on the fly and may never be seen again.

If you are approaching application servers as a Webmaster, you are used to the constant changes on a Web site; what you may not be used to is the IT standards for building systems, and that is what you are now doing. Conversely, if you are approaching application servers from the IT side, you may be used to a more structured (and slower!) life than that found on the Web.

This chapter provides some tips to help you design your application server system for easy maintenance.

Problems Will Occur

It is tempting to think that your newly installed system will function perfectly until the end of time, but such is not the case. It is also tempting to think that users will follow instructinos, but that also is not the case.

When you complete the design of a system, you must turn around and try to pick holes in it. Some of those holes can be plugged with further development; however, others need to be dealt with as problems occur.

Some problems may seem incredible—how could anyone be so stupid? Before you allow yourself to say such things, remember that you, too, may have attempted to do two (or three!) things at once, and that while talking on the telephone you may have accidentally pressed the Enter key rather than the Delete key.

Documentation

Everything about the system should be documented. In the case of systems based on application servers, that is a daunting task: you have Web pages, database schemas, application server code (applets and servlets), and often a variety of third-party plug-ins and components.

It is easy to set up standards for documentation of all of these pieces of the system, but it is harder to actually generate the documentation and keep it up to date.

Make Documentation Automatic	The easiest way to make documentation correct is to make its generation automatic. Many application servers provide tools to manage their components; you can use them as basic documentation. Likewise, you will find documentation tools bundled with many database products. Unfortuantely, you may wind up with duplicate and inconsistent documentation. It is better to have less documentation covering all aspects of the system than spotty documentation about parts of it.
Document the Environment	Because so many pieces exist in application server-based systems, make certain that the entire environment is documented. You can do this in two ways:

1. You can keep track of what the environment consists of (operating systems, compilers, and so forth) at all times.

2. You can keep track of changes to the environment (installing a new compiler, for example). If you use an automated tool (like a database) to do this, you can convert the changes into a snapshot of the environment.

As you can see, it is essential that you keep track of every change that you make to the environment.

Keep the Documentation Safe (and Secure)	Having decided to document everything, you should remember that you have a blueprint to guide you—or anyone else—in recreating it. Your documentation should be perhaps the most secure document in your organization.

Likewise, be careful about your use of comments on Web pages. As noted previously, the source code of Web pages is easily viewed; a paragraph of comments about your system's architecture is a good idea—but probably not where the public can find it.

Design for the Long Term

In general, software lasts much longer than most people expect it to. Application servers represent an architecture more than a product; you will swap pieces of the architecture in and out over the years. Avoid tying the implementation of the system (or any part of it) to idiosyncratic designs, specific people, or individual vendors. That will provide the most stable environment.

It should not come as a great surprise to you that many vendors will give you contradictory advice. Tying your system design to their unique products provides them with a reliable cash flow—and may give you some benefits when it comes to integration. Remember, though, that many, many systems outlive their support products.

Integration of Business Logic and Operations

A very serious problem arises in the management of Web sites—particularly of sites powered by application servers. The operations of the site are initially defined by management and designers; the operations are implemented by engineers, Web page designers, and programmers. In many cases (not all), when the project is finished and goes live, everything is in synch.

How Problems Arise	Over time, however, the maintenance of the site can cause the two to diverge. Since the site does in fact operate the business, this divergence means that the definition of the operation devolves to the engineers, Web page designers, and programmers. While this can be empowering, it can be inappropriate, and it may expose senior management (even boards of directors) to charges of lack of due diligence in oversight.

These divergences most often arise in two ways:

1. The details of operations—particularly of exception conditions—are rarely specified in basic plans. Programmers very frequently make these decisions. This problem can arise even during initial development.

2. Over time, modifications to the system can change the way in which it operates. These changes—a normal part of maintenance—need to be tracked.

Preventing and Solving the Maintenance Problem	There really is only one good solution to these problems, and that is to integrate the business and technical parts of your operations. This does not mean that the chief executive officer needs to learn programming, nor does it mean that your software engineers need to learn marketing. However, it does mean that everyone needs to understand the objectives of the other party.

It also means that all parties need to understand that systems evolve and that new combinations of events emerge with the passage of time. The fact that the system was not designed to handle a specific condition is something that needs to be addressed: recriminations and finger-pointing do not help. Management needs to understand this evolution and that they will be called upon to revisit policy issues in software from time to time. Technical staffs need to understand that these newly discovered wrinkles and glitches are a normal part of even the best systems.

You can, of course, attempt to foresee every eventuality and not start work until everyone has signed off (in blood!) on every contingency and subcontingency. That is precisely the design methodology that has produced, bloated, late, and over-budget systems for the last half century. Watchfulness and flexibility are the key to surviving in today's world; fortunately the architecture of application servers makes it possible to react quickly to the new challenges you discover.

Summary

Documentation—or more often, the absence of documentation—is often the difference between a successful system and one that struggles from one disaster to the next. Recognizing that documentation is essential is not enough: using the strategies outlined in this chapter to make documentation automatic and to recognize that problems will occur can help your system succeed.

When problems do occur, it is important to know about them and react to them quickly. Feedback is the topic of the next chapter.

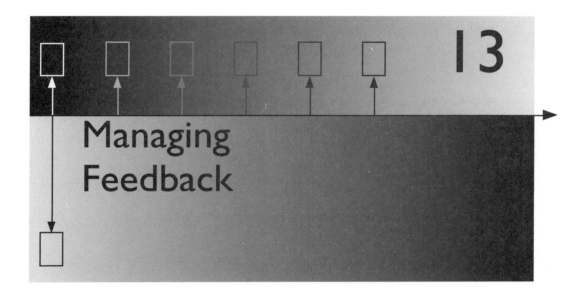

Managing
Feedback

Manging feedback does not just mean answering panic calls: it means being able to identify problems and then to deal with them efficiently and effectively without having to create a new procedure each time.

If you are new to the world of 24x7 operations, this may be a totally new adventure. In the corporate IT world, many systems run overnight, and people are used to being awakened at home to deal with problems. However there is a known schedule—end-of-day processing runs at night, not at mid-day. In the world of the Internet, everything may run all the time—there may be no respite.

If you are from the world of the Web, you may not be used to the demands of the traditional IT world. "Under construction" is not ac-

ceptable on the checkout page of an e-commerce site. Things have to work. Now.

Here are some key areas to consider in deploying an application server-based system.

Identifying Problems

Make certain that you can identify problems quickly. This may sound absurdly simple, but one of the most frequently heard complaints from users of computer systems is that when they call the hotline for help, they are told "Nothing is wrong."

Frequently, users are the first to know about a problem. You need to develop a call-screening mechanism that can pick up the slightest variation in requests for assistance and raise a red flag that something may be wrong. (There is help desk software available for this.)

Despite the fact that users often are the first to know of a problem, they often misidentify and misdiagnose problems. Take all of the input that you can get and assemble it—but question it. Indeed, the user may get a message, "Invalid password," but that may arise from a garbled user ID on the previous screen.

One key aspect of identifying problems is keeping track of them. You should never diagnose the same problem twice. Use help desk software or your own problem database to assist you.

If you have a database of problems, you can often ease your support burden by making it available to your users. Many people are reluctant to do this for a variety of reasons; however, in the long run it often does save time and effort in support and even redevelopment costs.

Setting Up the Feedback Loop

Since users are frequently the first to spot a problem, how do they get in touch with you? Set up the feedback loop at the beginning of your project; incorporate it into the design.

If you expect people to send you e-mail with bug reports, make certain that the e-mail link is available on all Web pages. You can consider building a small Perl script or Java applet to automate the production of the e-mail message and to provide information (date, time, which page is currently displayed, and so forth).

Like documentation, this is not something that you can add on at the end: it must be designed in from the start.

Acting on Feedback

Once you have set up your feedback loop, you need to act on it. To whom is the e-mail addressed? Who answers the phone? Expectations of immediate response are very high among users of the Web (and of all contemporary computer systems). You need a mechanism that is responsive at all times.

One way of handling responsiveness is to set up e-mail forwarding so that messages go to a variety of people, one of whom is always available (presumably). A problem with e-mail forwarding is that people often forget that it is active, and the messages wind up getting lost.

Test your feedback system and monitor it. If on a normal day you get 4 e-mail messages with queries or problems, check into things if you get none for 2 days.

Most important, know who is responsible for feedback. There is the direct responsibility of those who answer phone calls and e-mail messages as well as the managerial responsibility of those who must make certain that everything runs smoothly. Try to avoid the mindset that feedback is a bad thing. Certainly errors in code are not good, but if you try to hide them or explain them away (rather than fixing them), your system's integrity and quality will suffer.

Acting on External Matters

Finally, remember that in most cases your application server-based system is not the center of the universe. The application server architecture is designed modularly so that components can be replaced and changes made easily.

If you are working with an enterprise-wide database, that database may change in a variety of ways that affect your system. If you are using abstractions such as ODBC and JDBC, you may be able to maintain your logical view of the database and map it to the changed database. But if you do need to make changes, remember that one of the primary design objectives is the ability to make changes. So do not resent having to do so.

Finally, remember that the world may change. One company may merge with another, systems may need to be modified, and so forth. If you want to write a system, turn it on, and then go away, today's world of computing is not for you.

Summary

Your site will not be perfect. Problems will happen, and users will misunderstand the apparently clear instructions and information that you provide. Developing appropriate feedback mechanisms can nip potential problems in the bud.

Now that you have seen what the world of application servers is all about, one question may still be on your mind: how can you use these technologies yourself? The last chapter addresses that issue.

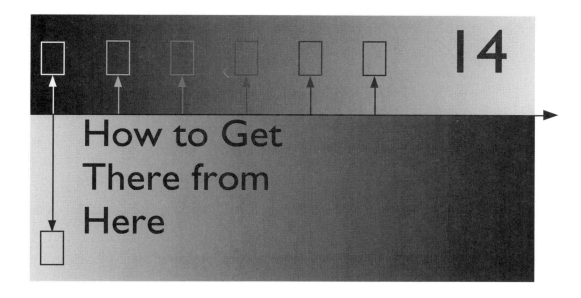

How to Get There from Here

The world of application servers—the world of interoperable systems, replaceable components, databases, and the Web—is here today. Its obvious benefits with regard to cost of development and speed of deployment are clear. How can you move into that world?

This chapter describes some of the key steps you can take. First, you need to know where you are—what sort of computing environment you have. Next, you need to know what you want to do. And finally, you need a plan for getting there.

Where Are You Now?

Unless you are a start-up company, you have systems, people, and operations in place today. Rushing ahead without concern for the status quo is always a risky endeavor.

Systems

Legacy code may be able to be converted to an application server-based system. You will most likely be able to strip out hundreds of lines of custom-written code that handles functionality such as transactions, concurrency, and telecommunications. What is left will be what is most valuable: your organization's business logic.

Unfortunately, all of this may be intertwined together, and it may be impossible to separate apparently routine telecommunications processing from idiosyncratic operations. (It is not unknown, for example, to find a little utility that converts between ASCII and EBCDIC character sets—and that also rejiggers customer ID numbers from one format to another.)

As you take the existing systems apart, you may find code that appears to be (and is) wrong. Many organizations have discovered such bugs as they perform the ultimate code review (dismantling). At this point, you have a choice: fix the code (and "break" the system), or modify the business logic.

One of the biggest hurdles you need to face is the fact that the interactivity of older types of systems is not present on the Web, which is primarily stateless. This impacts all aspects of a system. The give and take of a truly interactive system over a responsive private network is sluggish and a little peculiar over the Web. The emphasis in Web-based systems is on designs that prevent errors, rather than responsive error messages.

People

You have an investment in people—users who are trained in using the existing systems as well as your staff (in-house and consultants) who maintain it. Moving to a new architecture requires a significant amount of retraining for your support staff; moving to a new type of interface can require a significant amount of user retraining.

The good part of this, however, is that you are moving to industry standard interfaces and architectures. The user who needed two days of specialized training to learn which function keys to push on a dumb terminal may well be able to learn how to use a Web-based interface with minimal specialized training.

This is one of the reasons why many organizations encourage their staffs—within limits—to aggressively use the Web, even for non-business-related activities.

Operations

Because the architecture of application servers is fairly well defined in most environments, it may be more structured than your current operations. As with your code, you may find that your telecommunications support staff is intertwined in business operations. Unravelling operations may be as complicated as unravelling code.

What Do You Want to Do?

As your organization evolves, its systems, people, and operations may change. What changes do you anticipate?

Systems

Application server architecture provides a way of implementing a system that can work on a single personal computer, a mainframe, or some combination. Moving to application server architecture is a commitment to the architecture, not to a specific hardware or software configuration. This is much of its allure.

Notwithstanding the fact that application server architecture allows you great flexibility, you should have an idea of what you want to do with your systems. The biggest choice for many organizations today is what systems they want to develop and maintain in-house and which ones they want to move to vendors (or be able to move to vendors in the future).

People

The biggest consequence of moving to application servers may be in your staff—both software developers and support staffs. By centralizing business logic in the application server, you will find that you need people with domain-specific knowledge (knowledge of your business operations) and a reasonable grasp of the operations of the application server.

However, you will find that the people working on the interface may need much less knowledge of the underlying software than they do today. That is simply because the underlying software—Web technology—is so pervasive and so many people are familiar with it.

By the same token, your telecommunications staff may no longer deal at all with users: they may need no domain-specific knowledge. In fact, if you are moving to a Web-based system, you may have no support for users: they may all be using Internet service providers to access your system.

Operations	Moving to an application server-based environment has a significant impact on operations. For one, it allows you to distribute your computer operations both internally and externally. Since the interfaces between the components are so clearly defined, it is quite feasible to have your database running on a corporate data center, your Web server and application server running in a colocated operation at a vendor, and your network operations farmed out to a variety of ISPs.

In looking at your environment, consider your organization's objectives. Is more centralization in the offing? Are you looking to decentralize and offload some operations?

Planning for Application Servers

Depending on where you are and what you want to do, you have a number of choices in implementing application servers. For many organizations, implementing a small non-critical system on a small application server (even on a single personal computer) is a good way to get started.

For others, moving to an application server based on existing in-house technology (such as an existing Web server or database), can be a profitable way of working. Remember that the task is not particularly complicated—especially if you remember that architecture outlined in this book; however, it is likely to be a little more complicated than your vendor may suggest.

Yet another way of getting started with application servers is purchasing an integrated vertical market system that relies on this architecture. Such products are increasing available as specialized system vendors realize that they can actually make more money by producing a smaller product (that is, the application server/business logic) than by producing a soup-to-nuts total environment with support for databases and telecommunications.

Summary

Application server technology lets you implement dynamic Web sites from scratch. More important, application server technology lets you implement dynamic Web sites from the environment you now have: from legacy systems, a variety of databases, and an assortment of computers.

This is the appeal of application servers: not only do they work, but they provide a simple bridge to the future for the systems of the past. Their reliance on industry-wide standards for interfaces and protocols means that components can be swapped in and out. That twenty-year-old database, for example, can be replaced by a spiffy new one—provided that both comply with ODBC or JDBC standards. A TP monitor can balance your site's load over a single computer (not too hard to do) as well as over a collection of a dozen mainframes (as your business grows).

In *Database-Driven Web Sites*, you saw the opportunities for integrating databases with Web sites as well as how to do it on a small scale. In this book, you have seen how application servers can make that integration successful on a larger scale. Together, the books cover what you need to know about creating and maintaining a modern Web site that can support static and dynamic information as well as the transactions essential for e-commerce. All that is left is to manage the whole operation. That is the topic of the third book in this series, *Managing the Web-Based Enterprise*.

Application Servers Today

As noted throughout this book, application servers are evolving rapidly—through development as well as merger activity among the companies involved. The underlying technologies are stable (albeit not fully implemented in some cases). This appendix provides a snapshot of application servers today with the features that they contain. It is as accurate as possible; an online version of the database behind this chapter is available at http://www.philmontmill.com.

How This Data Was Assembled

As this book was being written, the world of application servers grew both in terms of the number of products on the market and in the scope of those products. All of the major vendors who had products in the market—both shipping and announced but not yet shipping—were contacted and asked to complete a questionnaire. The results of those questionnaires are given in this appendix. (The information contained here as well as updates to these and other products can be found on the Web at http://www.philmontmill.com.)

The information provided below is presented "as is" based on the vendors' information with only minor edits related to spelling, punctuation, and style. In an attempt to be impartial, the products are presented in alphabetical order. Notes and comments are those of the vendors unless otherwise indicated.

No product was excluded from this list by the author; a few vendors chose not to respond.

The major vendors who are missing are Sun, Netscape, and Microsoft. In the case of Sun and Netscape, their application server products were being merged at the time of publication, and information was not available on the new product's features. In the case of Microsoft, they made it clear that they wished to be included. However, as press time approached, they provided no information and did not return messages from the author and the editor.

The questionnaire was primarily a multiple-choice document with plenty of room for comments and notes. The entry in the next section shows the questionnaire in its entirety. The individual products follow.

Do not think that more features are necessarily better and rate products accordingly. Look for features that you need for the task that you need to perform and to properly interact with existing software and databases.

QUESTIONNAIRE

Vendor Information

Vendor

Contact

URL

Description   This description (as all the information in this section) is provided by the vendor. Minor copy edits have been made.

Production Environment

For more information on the production environment, see Chapter 4, "Sub-Programs and Application Servers" starting on page 85.

Platforms   AIX
               AS/400
               Digital Unix
               HP-UX
               Irix
               Mac OS (includes Carbon, etc.)
               NetWare
               SGI

	Solaris
	Windows NT
Web Servers	Any CGI supporting Web Server
	Apache
	IBM HTTP Server
	Lotus Domino
	Microsoft Internet Information Server
	Netscape
	Self-Contained (no other Web Server needed)
	Spyglass
Connections	NSAPI
	MSAPI
	ISAPI
	CGI

Notes for the environment are sometimes provided by the vendor.

Development Environment

The development environment is discussed in Chapter 5, "Components, Objects, and Application Servers" starting on page 99.

Languages Supported	C
	C++
	Cobol
	CORBA
	Java
	LiveHTML
	Objective C
	Perl
	Proprietary Basic
	Smalltalk
	Visual Basic

Notes for the development environment are sometimes provided by the vendor.

Object Environment

For more information on the object environment, see Chapter 7, "Connecting to Logic: COM, CORBA, EJB, and RMI" starting on page 127.

ORB

COM/CORBA/IIOP
CORBA
CORBA/IIOP
DCOM
Java/EJB
RMI/IIOP
RMI/JRMP

Component Models

COM/DCOM
CORBA
EJB

Notes for the object environment are sometimes provided by the vendor.

Database Environment

The database environment is discussed in Chapter 8, "Connecting to Data: ODBC and JDBC" starting on page 147.

ADO (ActiveX Data Objects)
DB2
Informix
JDBC
Microsoft
ODBC
OLE DB

Oracle
PL/SQL
SQL Server
Sybase

Notes for the database environment are sometimes provided by the vendor.

Transaction Environment

The transaction environment is discussed in Chapter 9, "Transaction Processing and TP Monitors" starting on page 157.

CORBA OTS (Open Transaction Standard)
External TP Monitors
Java Transaction Service (JTS)
MTS (Microsoft Transaction Server)
Whatever the HTTP Server Supports
X/Open XA and TX

Notes for the transaction environment are sometimes provided by the vendor.

Security Environment

Security is explored in Chapter 10, "Security and Application Servers" starting on page 173.

ACL
LDAP
SSL 3.0
Whatever the HTTP Server Supports
X.509 certificates

Notes for the security environment are sometimes provided by the vendor.

Interface Environment

See Chapter 6, "Developing the Interface" starting on page 111 for more information on the interface environment.

ASP
JSP
XML

Interface Notes: Notes for the interface environment are sometimes provided by the vendor.

Other

Management Tools and Development Environment

Information about management tools and the development environment was also solicited.

Finally, other notes and information are provided by some of the vendors.

COLDFUSION SERVER

Vendor Information

Vendor   Allaire Corporation

URL   http://www.allaire.com

Contact	Allaire Corporation One Alewife Center Cambridge, MA 02140 Phone: 617-761-2000 Fax: 617-761-2001 e-mail: info@allaire.com
Description	ColdFusion Server is part of the ColdFusion development platform, providing rapid, scalable, open application development and deployment.

Production Environment

For more information on the production environment, see Chapter 4, "Sub-Programs and Application Servers" starting on page 85.

Platforms	HP-UX Solaris Windows NT
Web Servers	Any CGI supporting Web Server, Apache, Microsoft Internet Information Server, Netscape
Connections	CGI ISAPI MSAPI NSAPI

Development Environment

The development environment is discussed in Chapter 5, "Components, Objects, and Application Servers" starting on page 99.

Languages Supported	C C++ CORBA Java Third party extensions exist for Visual Basic and Delphi languages.

Object Environment

For more information on the object environment, see Chapter 7, "Connecting to Logic: COM, CORBA, EJB, and RMI" starting on page 127.

ORB	COM/CORBA/IIOP CORBA CORBA/IIOP DCOM Java/EJB
Component Models	COM/DCOM CORBA EJB

Database Environment

The database environment is discussed in Chapter 8, "Connecting to Data: ODBC and JDBC" starting on page 147.

ADO
DB2
Informix
Microsoft
ODBC
OLE DB
Oracle
SQL Server
Sybase

Transaction Environment

The transaction environment is discussed in Chapter 9, "Transaction Processing and TP Monitors" starting on page 157.

MTS (Microsoft Transaction Server)
Whatever the HTTP server supports

Security Environment

Security is explored in Chapter 10, "Security and Application Servers" starting on page 173.

LDAP
SSL 3.0
X.509 Certificates
Whatever the HTTP server supports

Interface Environment

See Chapter 6, "Developing the Interface" starting on page 111 for more information on the interface environment.

JSP
XML

Other

Management Tools and Development Environment	ColdFusion Studio (IDE)

EASERVER

Vendor Information

Vendor	Sybase
URL	www.sybase.com
Contact	e-mail: sales@sybase.com
Description	Enterprise Application Server provides the high performance, productive, secure, and flexible platform essential for Web-enabling your back office systems. It is based on proven Sybase application server technology, Open Server, which is used to run thousands of successfully deployed applications around the world. EAServer also features seamless integration with Sybase PowerJ and PowerBuilder, but can be used with components developed with a wide variety of Java, C++, and COM development tools. It provides the comprehensive security features essential when providing access to applications from beyond the firewall. Finally, EAServer is built on open standards such

as CORBA, Java, COM, ODBC, and JDBC to provide an open and flexible environment you can trust to support you into the future.

Production Environment

For more information on the production environment, see Chapter 4, "Sub-Programs and Application Servers" starting on page 85.

Platforms
AIX
Solaris
Windows NT

Web Servers
Apache
Microsoft Internet Information Server
Netscape
Self-contained (no other Web Server)

Connections
CGI
ISAPI
NSAPI

Development Environment

The development environment is discussed in Chapter 5, "Components, Objects, and Application Servers" starting on page 99.

Languages Supported
C
C++
CORBA
Java
Also supported are PowerBuilder, Java (EJB and Servlets)

Object Environment

For more information on the object environment, see Chapter 7, "Connecting to Logic: COM, CORBA, EJB, and RMI" starting on page 127.

ORB

COM/CORBA/IIOP
CORBA
CORBA/IIOP
DCOM
Java/EJB

Component
Models

COM/DCOM
CORBA
EJB

Database Environment

The database environment is discussed in Chapter 8, "Connecting to Data: ODBC and JDBC" starting on page 147.

DB2
Oracle
Informix
JDBC
SQL Server
Microsoft
Sybase
ODBC

Transaction Environment

The transaction environment is discussed in Chapter 9, "Transaction Processing and TP Monitors" starting on page 157.

CORBA OTS
MTS (Microsoft Transaction Server)

Security Environment

Security is explored in Chapter 10, "Security and Application Servers" starting on page 173.

SSL 3.0
X.509 Certificates
Also Verisign and Entrust certificates. Also OS and Customer authentication. Users can be placed into roles for accessing packages or components.

Interface Environment

See Chapter 6, "Developing the Interface" starting on page 111 for more information on the interface environment.

ASP
XML

Other

**Management and
Development
Tools**

Enterprise Application Server provides easy runtime management, with the ability to:

- manage the server,

- manage database connections,

- monitor runtime activity,

- monitor server clusters, and

- view log files.

This is provided via Sybase Central.
Tightly integrated with Sybase's development tools. These tools include PowerBuilder, PowerJ, and PowerSite.

GALILEO APPLICATION SERVER

Vendor Information

Vendor   Esemplare Development

URL   www.esemplare.com

Contact   Esemplare Development
                 32 Monsey Place
                 Staten Island, NY 10303
                 Phone: 718-698-0070
                 e-mail: sales@esemplare.com

Description   Galileo is a fully scalable and platform independent development system which allows the creation of database-driven Web applications using custom HTML tags. It has been designed to simplify the design, development, deployment, and maintenance of Web based applications.
                 Since Galileo was written in Java, it will run on any platform that supports the Java Virtual Machine, including Windows 95/98, Windows NT, SPARC Solaris, HP-UX, and Linux.
                 And best of all, Galileo is FREE to use.

Production Environment

For more information on the production environment, see Chapter 4, "Sub-Programs and Application Servers" starting on page 85.

Platforms

AIX
Digital Unix
HP-UX
Irix
Mac OS (includes Carbon etc.)
NetWare
SGI
Solaris
Windows NT

Web Servers

Apache
IBM HTTP Server
Lotus Domino
Microsoft Internet Information Server
Netscape
Spyglass

Connections

ISAPI
MSAPI
NSAPI

Development Environment

The development environment is discussed in Chapter 5, "Components, Objects, and Application Servers" starting on page 99.

Languages Supported

Java

Object Environment

For more information on the object environment, see Chapter 7, "Connecting to Logic: COM, CORBA, EJB, and RMI" starting on page 127.

ORB   CORBA
Java/EJB

Component   CORBA
Models   EJB

Database Environment

The database environment is discussed in Chapter 8, "Connecting to Data: ODBC and JDBC" starting on page 147.

DB2
Informix
JDBC
Microsoft
ODB
Oracle
SQL Server
Sybase

Transaction Environment

The transaction environment is discussed in Chapter 9, "Transaction Processing and TP Monitors" starting on page 157.

Whatever the HTTP server supports

Security Environment

Security is explored in Chapter 10, "Security and Application Servers" starting on page 173.

Whatever the HTTP server supports

Interface Environment

See Chapter 6, "Developing the Interface" starting on page 111 for more information on the interface environment.

XML

Other

Management and Development Tools   Built-in web interface for easy management

GEMSTONE/J APPLICATION SERVER FOR JAVA

Vendor Information

Vendor   GemStone Systems, Inc.

URL	http://www.gemstone.com
Contact	GemStone Systems, Inc. 20575 NW von Neumann Drive Beaverton, OR 97006 Phone: 503-533-3000; 800-243-9369 Fax: 503-629-8556 e-mail: info@gemstone.com
Description	GemStone/J 3.0 is the most secure application platform for business-to-business Internet commerce applications built in Java. The Gem-Stone/J 3.0 application server provides a robust foundation that meets the demanding requirements for security, scalability, performance, and reliability that are the keys to success in Internet commerce environments. GemStone/J 3.0 is based on Java 2 Enterprise Edition (J2EE) technologies including Java 2, Java Security Architecture, JavaServer Pages (JSP), Java Servlets and Enterprise JavaBeans. GemStone/J 3.0 integrates these Java components with an all-Java CORBA ORB for interoperability and an Object Transaction Monitor (OTM) to enable coordinated business transaction processing. GemStone/J 3.0's unique Persistent Cache Architecture (PCA) is key to providing high performance and coordinated business transactions for Internet commerce applications. GemStone/J 3.0's open architecture supports a wide choice of development tools, components, Web servers, client browsers, and databases.

Production Environment

For more information on the production environment, see Chapter 4, "Sub-Programs and Application Servers" starting on page 85.

Platforms	Solaris Windows NT
Web Servers	Apache

Microsoft Internet Information Server
Netscape

Connections   NSAPI

Development Environment

The development environment is discussed in Chapter 5, "Components, Objects, and Application Servers" starting on page 99.

Languages   CORBA
Supported   Java
GemStone/J 3.0 supports a tools-independent, open development environment. It supports all leading Java IDEs, including Symantec Visual Café, IBM VisualAge for Java, and INPRISE JBuilder. After new applications are developed in an IDE, GemStone/J's tool set, which includes the GemStone/J Deployer and Debugger, allows the developer to deploy, optimize, and manage these applications in GemStone/J. The GemStone/J Deployer creates the necessary EJB infrastructure (artifacts) required for deployment of new EJB applications. Developers use the GemStone/J Debugger to debug applications before and after they are deployed into the GemStone/J environment.

Object Environment

For more information on the object environment, see Chapter 7, "Connecting to Logic: COM, CORBA, EJB, and RMI" starting on page 127.

ORB   CORBA
          CORBA/IIOP
          Java/EJB

Component Models

CORBA
EJB
GemStone/J has a fully transactional persistent cache architecture (PCA) that supplies the necessary component infrastructure for component models (transactional, shared object cache) on the middle tier in addition to fully supporting relational data-of-record that may exist in RDBMSs.

Database Environment

The database environment is discussed in Chapter 8, "Connecting to Data: ODBC and JDBC" starting on page 147.

DB2
Informix
JDBC
Oracle
PL/SQL
SQL Server

GemStone/J provides high volume and high performance connectivity with third–tier data using standard Java interfaces. With built-in JDBC drivers, GemStone/J integrates with a wide variety of relational databases and platform configurations, including UNIX, NT, and mainframe platforms. Mainframe connectivity is supported through standard Java/CORBA interfaces and MQSeries.

GemStone/J supports the latest O/R mapping technology. O/R mapping tools convert third-party relational data into object data for use by a Java application with less developer interaction.

Using 2-phase commit and Persistent Cache, GemStone/J provides both tightly and loosely coupled synchronization policies to third-tier data. The ability to loosely synchronize between the middle and third tier means the system does not have to communicate every transaction immediately to the third tier. It can wait and do transactions in batches.

Other capabilities include:

- Configurable JDBC connection pools

- Concurrent access to multiple RDBMSs

- Small JDBC footprint

- Security into RDBMSs

- Secure Socket Layer into the RDBMSs

- Integration with GemStone/J OTM 2-phase distributed transactions and recovery

- 100% Pure Java interface

Transaction Environment

The transaction environment is discussed in Chapter 9, "Transaction Processing and TP Monitors" starting on page 157.

CORBA OTS

Java Transaction Service (JTS)

With the GemStone/J all-Java Object Transaction Monitor (OTM), both developers and administrators benefit from the simplicity, consistency, and efficiency of an integrated Java transaction monitor. The GemStone/J OTM gives developers a standard infrastructure with which they can build component-based applications that are fully transactional and that work with multiple databases.

With the GemStone/J OTM, developers build EJB or CORBA applications that can initiate or participate in 2-phase, XA-compliant, fully recoverable transactions with relational databases and with GemStone/J's Persistent Cache. The GemStone/J OTM performs transactions against Java objects in the Persistent Cache and third-tier data of record (relational data, packaged software applications, and mainframes). Cache coherency between the Persistent Cache and relational databases is maintained with the GemStone/J OTM.

The GemStone/J OTM incorporates an Object Transaction Service (OTS) 1.1 implementation with a Java Transaction Service (JTS) Java binding. This implementation includes an OTS 1.1 Synchronization interface. Both the ORB and OTS are implemented in Java and are designed to work with GemStone/J's EJB container and server. GemStone/J EJB applications can exploit the productivity of Java components without compromising the interoperability and integrity that comes from using established transaction processing monitor and CORBA standards. The GemStone/J OTM also interoperates with other OTS implementations.

Security Environment

Security is explored in Chapter 10, "Security and Application Servers" starting on page 173.

ACL
LDAP
SSL 3.0
X.509 Certificates

GemStone/J security is Java 2-based and is extended to meet the expectations of enterprise-class application developers. The security GemStone/J offers includes not only code-based security but also user-level and method-level security, including full support of the method-level security specified by EJB. User-level security is implemented using standard X.509 digital certificates and Access Control Lists (ACLs), controlling and restricting user access to various system-wide resources. Secure communication and encryption is fully supported through Secure Socket Layer (SSL) and standard ciphersuites. End-to-end security embedded into GemStone/J's Persistent Cache Architecture (PCA) technology and OTM supply a powerful security infrastructure, giving the developer authentication, authorization, secure communication, and security administration. Authentication and authorization checks throughout the system include the use of ACLs for both users and groups, SSL for communication, and security administration through Console tools and utilities. The developer can now focus on application logic and leave the security infrastructure to GemStone/J. All the security embedded into GemStone/J is based on security standards from Sun Microsystems and industry standards. The Java security standards for Java 2 (JSA, JCA, and JCE) and EJB are fully supported and extended through the industry standards of Public Key Infrastructure (PKI), X.509 certificates, X.500 names, and SSL 3.0. Standard ciphersuites are supported as well for both domestic and international applications.

Interface Environment

See Chapter 6, "Developing the Interface" starting on page 111 for more information on the interface environment.

JSP
XML

For effective Internet scalability, GemStone/J provides a servlet engine that supports JSP and Java Servlets. Companies deploying applications this year will be able to handle peak loads of tens of thousands of concurrent users with this technology. GemStone/J supplies high-end client scalability through the servlet engine and its integration with Web servers to provide access to Web browsers on the Internet as well as direct connections through CORBA and Java interfaces for CORBA and Java clients.

Integrated into the GemStone/J VM, the servlet engine takes advantage of the Persistent Cache Architecture to support session pooling and distributed HTTP session state and load-balancing capabilities to deliver a robust runtime environment. Because the servlet runs in the servlet engine, it has access to all of GemStone/J's services.

All clients can access EJB applications using one persistent global naming service and native CORBA and Java interfaces. GemStone/J supports all Java clients and standard Web browsers, including Netscape Navigator and Microsoft Internet Explorer. Web servers supported by GemStone/J include Netscape's Enterprise and FastTrack Web Servers, Apache Web Server, and Microsoft IIS Web Server.

Other

Management and Development Tools

Use our IDE position on supporting IDEs of your choice in an open development environment.

Features

- Complete Java 2 security implementation
- Highly scalable Web integration makes use of JavaServer Pages and Java Servlet technologies
- Persistent Cache stores up to 2 billion objects
- Robust Enterprise JavaBeans implementation
- Open development environment supports your choice of development tools

HAHTSITE APPLICATION SERVER

Vendor Information

Vendor   HAHTsite

URL   http://www.haht.com

Contact   Phone: 1-888-GET-HAHT
                e-mail : info@haht.com

Description   The HAHTsite Application Server provides massive scalability, enter-
                prise-level security, and unmatched openness and flexibility for both
                Java and Microsoft infrastructures. Its distributed architecture and high
                availability features ensure 24X7 delivery of enterprise applications to
                an unlimited number of users.

                The HAHTsite Integrated Development Environment manages the
                complexity of creating enterprise applications and speeds develop-
                ment by automating many tasks performed by developers and con-
                tent creators.

Production Environment

For more information on the production environment, see Chapter 4, "Sub-Programs
and Application Servers" starting on page 85.

Platforms   AIX
                HP-UX
                Solaris
                Windows NT

Web Servers	Any CGI supporting Web Server Apache Microsoft Internet Information Server Netscape
Connections	CGI ISAPI MSAPI NSAPI

Development Environment

The development environment is discussed in Chapter 5, "Components, Objects, and Application Servers" starting on page 99.

Languages Supported	Java Visual Basic

HAHTsite allows one to develop applications using Java or HAHTtalk Basic, a non-proprietary, 100% Visual Basic compliant language.

Object Environment

For more information on the object environment, see Chapter 7, "Connecting to Logic: COM, CORBA, EJB, and RMI" starting on page 127.

EJB support is planned for a future release. Availability planned in Q2/2000. We will have Servlet support by end of 1999.

ORB	COM/CORBA/IIOP CORBA CORBA/IIOP DCOM RMI/JRMP

Component Models	COM/DCOM CORBA EJB

Database Environment

The database environment is discussed in Chapter 8, "Connecting to Data: ODBC and JDBC" starting on page 147.

ADO
DB2
Informix
JDBC
Microsoft
ODBC
OLE DB
Oracle
SQL Server
Sybase

Transaction Environment

The transaction environment is discussed in Chapter 9, "Transaction Processing and TP Monitors" starting on page 157.

External TP Monitors
MTS (Microsoft Transaction Server)

HAHTsite provides Enterprise Solution Modules (ESMs) for rapid, easy access to TP Monitors such as BEA Tuxedo and IBM CICS. HAHTsite's native support for COM/DCOM makes calling out to MTS a simple task.

Security Environment

Security is explored in Chapter 10, "Security and Application Servers" starting on page 173.

ACL
LDAP
SSL 3.0
Whatever the HTTP server supports

HAHTsite also provides an ESM for Novell Directory Services and en-Commerce's getAccess. The product also provides its own internal role-based security mechanism.

Interface Environment

See Chapter 6, "Developing the Interface" starting on page 111 for more information on the interface environment.

XML

HAHTsite will support any web-based client using HTTP, or non-web clients using CORBA/IIOP or RMI/JRMP. XML is also supported. Servlet support will be provided by the end of the year, with EJB support following.

Other

Management and Development Tools

Product provides a web-based management console for the administration of clusters of application servers. The IDE and Application Server are tightly integrated and provide a unique one-button deployment mechanism, whereby applications can be deployed to multiple application servers with a single push of a button. The IDE also supports any SCC-API compliant source control environment for team development.

Features

The IDE is comparable with best of breed web development products in the market today. It provides support for Cascading Style sheets, WYSIWYG HTML editing, WYSIWYG Frames editing, WYSIWYG table-in-table editing, and the ability to embed application logic within HTML pages in a similar manner to JSPs (support planned shortly). The IDE also provides a variety of widgets and wizards for easy access to databases (via ADO:OLE DB or ODBC), and ERP systems such as SAP R/3 and PeopleSoft. HAHTsite's unique one-button deployment mechanism makes deploying applications a simple task. The Application Server provides support for a variety of features including full redundancy of all server components for high availability (fail-over support), phased shutdown support (the ability to mark an application server in a cluster for shutdown, only once all sessions are complete on the particular machine will the application server shut down), hot updates (application can be updated on the fly without having to bring the application server down), heterogeneous clusters (clusters can consist of a variety machines, all protocols are platform independent, seamless to developers), distributed configurations (application servers can be deployed behind firewalls for optimal security). HAHTsite also provides dynamic, weighted load balancing algorithms for optimal performance and page-level caching. Support for open standards includes CORBA (product is bundled with Inprise's VisiBroker ORB for Java, and COM/DCOM: both are supported natively, no bridges).

All applications are also compiled when deployed for optimal security (machine independent P-code for HAHTtalk Basic Applications, and .class files for Java Projects). Projects in the IDE can be partitioned and referred to for large project support and team development. A variety of ESMs are provided for access to other products including CICS, IMS TM, SAP R/3, PeopleSoft, Lotus Notes, LDAP, Novell Directory Services, Crystal Reports, and BEA Tuxedo. HAHT also provides the HAHTsite Integrated Publisher (IP), a lightweight version of the IDE suitable for content-creators.

INTERSTAGE

Vendor Information

Vendor   Fujitsu

Contact   e-mail: info@interstage.com

URL   www.interstage.com

Description   INTERSTAGE is a CORBA-based Application Server infrastructure
                  product which enables cross-platform and cross-language transaction-
                  al business logic implementation. It provides application development
                  and application deployment/execution environment on different
                  hardware/software platforms. It has C++/Java Application Server and
                  EJB Application Server core products and has multiple optional prod-
                  uct lines. As of today the optional product lines are 1. Legacy Gateway
                  and 2. Database Gateway.

                  INTERSTAGE core product and its optional product lines have inte-
                  grated distributed object technology (CORBA), Internet technology
                  (IETF), component technology (EJB), security and directory technolo-
                  gy, database technology, transaction processing technology (X/Open
                  DTP model, XA interface) and TP monitor systems (CICS, IMS, Tux-
                  edo), and asynchronous messaging system (MQSeries) and technolo-
                  gy in the application server infrastructure.

Production Environment

For more information on the production environment, see Chapter 4, "Sub-Programs and Application Servers" starting on page 85.

Platforms	Solaris
	Windows NT
Web Servers	Any CGI supporting Web Server
	IBM HTTP Server
	Microsoft Internet Information Server
	Netscape
Connections	CGI
	ISAPI
	NSAPI

Development Environment

The development environment is discussed in Chapter 5, "Components, Objects, and Application Servers" starting on page 99.

Languages Supported	C
	C++
	Cobol
	CORBA
	Java
	Visual Basic

Object Environment

For more information on the object environment, see Chapter 7, "Connecting to Logic: COM, CORBA, EJB, and RMI" starting on page 127.

ORB	COM/CORBA/IIOP
	CORBA
	CORBA/IIOP
	Java/EJB

RMI/IIOP
RMI/JRMP

Component
Models

COM/DCOM
CORBA
EJB

Database Environment

The database environment is discussed in Chapter 8, "Connecting to Data: ODBC and JDBC" starting on page 147.

ADO (ActiveX Data Objects)
DB2
Informix
JDBC
Microsoft
ODBC
Oracle
PL/SQL
SQL Server
Sybase

Transaction Environment

The transaction environment is discussed in Chapter 9, "Transaction Processing and TP Monitors" starting on page 157.

CORBA OTS (Open Transaction Standard)
External TP Monitors
Java Transaction Service (JTS)
X/Open XA and TX

Security Environment

Security is explored in Chapter 10, "Security and Application Servers" starting on page 173.

LDAP
SSL 3.0
X.509 certificates

Interface Environment

See Chapter 6, "Developing the Interface" starting on page 111 for more information on the interface environment.

JSP
XML

Other

Management Tools and Development Environment

Any third party CORBA/Java IDE

Features

CORBA
EJB
Legacy Gateway
Database Gateway

ORACLE APPLICATION SERVER

Vendor Information

Vendor   Oracle

URL   http://www.oracle.com/appserver/

Contact   Phone: 1-800-Oracle1

Description   As an integral part of the Oracle Internet Platform, Oracle Application Server's scalable, standards-based architecture and superior database integration are the foundation for supporting real-world applications in both corporate and e-business environments.

Production Environment

For more information on the production environment, see Chapter 4, "Sub-Programs and Application Servers" starting on page 85.

Platforms   AIX
                Digital Unix
                HP-UX
                Irix
                NetWare
                SGI
                SolarisWindows NT

Web Servers   Apache
                Microsoft Internet Information Server
                Netscape

	Self-contained (no other Web Server)
	Spyglass
Connections	CGI
	ISAPI
	MSAPI
	NSAPI

Development Environment

The development environment is discussed in Chapter 5, "Components, Objects, and Application Servers" starting on page 99.

Languages	C
Supported	C++
	Cobol
	CORBA
	Java
	LiveHTML
	Perl

Object Environment

For more information on the object environment, see Chapter 7, "Connecting to Logic: COM, CORBA, EJB, and RMI" starting on page 127.

ORB	CORBA
	CORBA/IIOP
	Java/EJB
Component	CORBA
Models	EJB

Database Environment

The database environment is discussed in Chapter 8, "Connecting to Data: ODBC and JDBC" starting on page 147.

DB2
Informix
JDBC
Microsoft
ODBC
Oracle
PL/SQL
SQL Server
Sybase

Can access any ODBC / JDBC compliant database including all the ones listed above. Rich connection pooling also available in an Oracle environment.

Transaction Environment

The transaction environment is discussed in Chapter 9, "Transaction Processing and TP Monitors" starting on page 157.

CORBA OTS
Java Transaction Service (JTS)
X/Open XA and TX

Security Environment

Security is explored in Chapter 10, "Security and Application Servers" starting on page 173.

LDAP
SSL 3.0

X.509 Certificates

Interface Environment

See Chapter 6, "Developing the Interface" starting on page 111 for more information on the interface environment.

ASP
JSP
XML

JSP support built in; ASP support available through third-party partner (ChiliSoft and Halcyon).

Other

Management and Development Tools

Built in browser-based managment tool which controls an entire site (may include multiple clustered appplication servers). Adding management capability to Oracle Enterprise Manager (to manage database, application server and applications from a single console).

Integration with third parties via SNMP.

Features

- Standards: EJBs, Servlet, JSPs, CORBA, IIOP

- Scalability / Reliability: Single server to distributed

- Development Choice: Java, Perl, C, C++, COBOL, PL/SQL

- Internet Platform: Integrated with database, tools, management

PROGRESS APPTIVITY 3.1

Vendor Information

Vendor   Progress Software Corporation

URL   www.apptivity.com

Description   Progress Apptivity is a Java application server with integrated develop-
                  ment environment for developing and deploying Web-based business
                  applications. Apptivity won first place for Java application servers test-
                  ed recently by *PC Week*, proving to be 50 to 100% faster than com-
                  petitive products. In addition, a recent GartnerGroup report from
                  placed Apptivity in the coveted "Leaders Quadrant" for Java integrat-
                  ed applications environments.

Production Environment

For more information on the production environment, see Chapter 4, "Sub-Programs
and Application Servers" starting on page 85.

Platforms   AIX
                  HP-UX
                  Solaris
                  Windows NT

Web Servers   Apache
                  Microsoft Internet Information Server
                  Netscape

Connections	Web pages served through standard servlet engine. Connection used depends on servlet engine chosen.

Development Environment

The development environment is discussed in Chapter 5, "Components, Objects, and Application Servers" starting on page 99.

Languages Supported	Java
	Includes: debugger, trace points, conditional breakpoints, IDE tools, visual/RAD tools, GUI builder, Java and HTML macros, configuration management, support for edit-compile-execute design cycle, JIT editor, JDK switching, servlet builder, remote debugger, internationalization support. Compliant with JDBC, JDK 2.0, Y2K.

Object Environment

For more information on the object environment, see Chapter 7, "Connecting to Logic: COM, CORBA, EJB, and RMI" starting on page 127.

ORB	CORBA
	CORBA/IIOP
	Java/EJB
Component Models	CORBA
	EJB

Database Environment

The database environment is discussed in Chapter 8, "Connecting to Data: ODBC and JDBC" starting on page 147.

JDBC

Transaction Environment

The transaction environment is discussed in Chapter 9, "Transaction Processing and TP Monitors" starting on page 157.

Supports standard JDBC transaction modes

Security Environment

Security is explored in Chapter 10, "Security and Application Servers" starting on page 173.

SSL 3.0

Interface Environment

See Chapter 6, "Developing the Interface" starting on page 111 for more information on the interface environment.

XML

Other

Management and Development Tools	Integrated Application Environment (IAE) and server management tools included.
Features	Auto-sensing page generation: targets HTML to specific browser, providing best display browser can support.
	New in Version 3.1: Support for XML, enhanced HTML and SQL functionality, provides for integration of business logic written for the large installed base of Progress 4GL applications.

SAPPHIRE/WEB

Vendor Information

Vendor	Bluestone Software
Contact	Bluestone Software
	Phone: 609-727-4600 or 1-888-bluestone
URL	www.bluestone.com

Description	The Sapphire/Web Application Server Framework Product Family addresses business needs by providing a robust, scalable, secure, flexible, and non-proprietary application server solution that addresses the four key parts of the software lifecycle: development, deployment, integration, and management.

Production Environment

For more information on the production environment, see Chapter 4, "Sub-Programs and Application Servers" starting on page 85.

Platforms	AIX AS/400 Digital Unix HP-UX Irix Mac OS (includes Carbon, etc.) NetWare SGI Solaris Windows NT
Web Servers	Any CGI supporting Web Server Apache IBM HTTP Server Lotus Domino Microsoft Internet Information Server Netscape Spyglass
Connections	NSAPI MSAPI ISAPI CGI

Sapphire/Web works with any web server and will deploy in any Java Virtual Machine on any platform.

Development Environment

The development environment is discussed in Chapter 5, "Components, Objects, and Application Servers" starting on page 99.

Languages Supported

C
C++
CORBA
Java

Object Environment

For more information on the object environment, see Chapter 7, "Connecting to Logic: COM, CORBA, EJB, and RMI" starting on page 127.

ORB

COM/CORBA/IIOP
Java/EJB

Component Models

COM/DCOM
CORBA
EJB

With Sapphire/Web you can deploy applications such as EJB, Servlet, Javabean, JSP. It comes with its own EJB server, but applications can run in any EJB server. Sapphire can integrate and dynamically introspect any Java distributed object.

Database Environment

The database environment is discussed in Chapter 8, "Connecting to Data: ODBC and JDBC" starting on page 147.

ADO (ActiveX Data Objects)
DB2
Informix
JDBC
Microsoft
ODBC
Oracle
SQL Server
Sybase

Transaction Environment

The transaction environment is discussed in Chapter 9, "Transaction Processing and TP Monitors" starting on page 157.

External TP Monitors

Sapphire supports single vendor database two phase commit transactions. It supports any transaction monitor for two phase commits across multiple vendor databases.

Security Environment

Security is explored in Chapter 10, "Security and Application Servers" starting on page 173.

ACL
LDAP
X.509 certificates

Interface Environment

See Chapter 6, "Developing the Interface" starting on page 111 for more information on the interface environment.

ASP
JSP
XML

Other

Management Tools and Development Environment

Sapphire/Developer: A mature, robust, flexible development environment. The key value propositions for Sapphire/Developer are:
• Increased developer productivity

• Shortened time to market for new applications.

• Decreased development costs and increased ROI on development time.

• Increased revenue: e-commerce applications can be deployed faster.

Sapphire/Universal Business Server (UBS): Application Server Framework

Our application server framework delivers value by providing a scalable, secure, high-volume Web application deployment architecture that adapts to new technologies as they become viable. The UBS delivers:
• Unlimited scalability: Businesses will not be locked into a technology that cannot meet the quality of service requirements of its customers, suppliers, and all enterprise stakeholders. As application popularity grows, scalability and performance become issues. Sapphire/Web's technology leadership and intrinsic ability to scale assure that customer/user quality of service requirements are met.

- Decreasing hardware costs: Sapphire/Web deploys 100% pure Java. As server-side Java becomes more prevalent, this capability means that businesses are not locked into any hardware platform. They are free to negotiate the best price for hardware without any software application dependencies.

- No Technology Lock-in: Sapphire/Web provides a deployment environment and services that deliver a high level of flexibility in operating systems, languages, database access and communication protocols. The value proposition for business is an improvement in process management. That is, now businesses will not be creating instant legacy applications.

Sapphire/Application Manager (SAM): An advanced management utility.

SAM delivers:
- Improved IT and process management: Single-source monitoring and control over entire Web infrastructure.

- Improved quality of service to customers: Assuring availability and performance of Web applications

Sapphire/EDK: Enterprise and Distributed Object Integration Component
- Improved organizational knowledge: By integrating with existing applications and providing compatibility with all distributed object models and specifications including EJB, CORBA, and COM/DCOM.

Sapphire/Integration Modules (SIMs): Pre-built Integration Modules
- Plug-and-play integrations to existing applications and IT infrastructures that allow organizations to leverage existing technology investments in applications like SAP, Peoplesoft, MQSeries, and CICS.

Features
- Sapphire is open: We provide everything you need, but also incorporate a "best-of-breed" philosophy. Integrate tools and technologies that your organization can be most productive with. Use any

client technology (HTML, Java, VB Script, JavaScript, XML, HDML, VRML).

• Multi-Mode IDE: Sapphire/Developer is designed to accommodate all types of users. With wizards, drag and drop, and code accessibility.

• Client-Object Framework: Pre-built sets of database access, graphing, charting, and client-side processing functionality using both Java or VBscript client technologies.

• Auto-Interface Generator: Generate Java or HTML user interfaces based on SQL.

• Object Repository: Team development capabilities.

• Import existing user interfaces: No need to rebuild everything.

• Bundled Java charting and graphing.

• SCCAPI compatibility: Sapphire/Web fits into any environment.

Deployment:

• Multiple Deployment Models: Sapphire/Web application servers can be deployed as Java EJB, Java Applications, Java Servlets, JavaBeans, C executables, C++ executables, CGI, ISAPI, NSAPI, Fast CGI, WRBAPI.

• EJB Server: Fully implemented EJB compliant server with swap-able JTS and JNDI.

• Persistent State Server: State Information can be in a database. In addition, state information can maintained forever by using state server object indexing.

• Independent State Server: Maintain state outside the application server if desired.

• Sun Certified 100% Pure Java: Run Sapphire/Web application servers in any JVM.

• XML Compatibility: XML client, content generators, SIM

• Optimal Weight Client Sensing: Determine client capabilities and zone content based on bandwidth.

- Application Isolation

Integration:

- Deploy applications using any communication protocol (HTTP, IIOP, DCOM, RMI SSL, SHTTP)

- Integrate COM and MTS objects, JavaBeans, EJBs, and CORBA

- Integrate and dynamically introspect any distributed object via its naming service

- Integrate CICS applications

- Integrate MQ Series and MSMQ SIMs

- Integrate Legacy applications via SNA to TCP/IP, or using 3270 emulation.

- Integrate any custom application programs and specific function objects

- Integrate SAP, PeopleSoft, PowerBuilder, and VB applications

- Integrate with LDAP

- Integrate with any source code control system

- Integrate any database (JDBC, Native, ODBC)

- Integrate Tuxedo transaction monitor

Management:

- Agent Based: Advanced agents monitor all components of the Web application server architecture.

- Management Console: Graphical user interface for drag and drop event coordination and discrepancy resolution.

- Event Logging: Log all interactions into database.

- Report Generation: Graphing, charting, and spreadsheet analysis of events.

- SMNP Integration: Route events to third-party system integration tools. Plug in advanced integration with CA Unicenter.

SYNERJ APPLICATION SERVER

Vendor Information

Vendor   Forte Software Inc.

URL   http://www.forte.com/

Contact   Forte Software Inc.
1800 Harrison Street
Oakland, CA 94612
email: info@forte.com

Description   SynerJ is a highly modular suite of development and deployment tools for assembling and creating applications, based entirely on the Java platform, that run on standard Java Virtual Machines (JVMs) with no proprietary runtime environment. The SynerJ Product Suite supports a "mix-and-match" solution, where any of the SynerJ products can be used with third-party Java products:

- SynerJ Application Server: Pure EJB 1.1 Container and Server

- SynerJ Developer: Repository driven IDE for creating Java applications

- SynerJ Assembler: Graphical EJB component assembly tool

Production Environment

For more information on the production environment, see Chapter 4, "Sub-Programs and Application Servers" starting on page 85.

Platforms	Solaris Windows NT
Web Servers	Any CGI supporting Web Server Apache Microsoft Internet Information Server Netscape
Connections	CGI ISAPI NSAPI

Development Environment

The development environment is discussed in Chapter 5, "Components, Objects, and Application Servers" starting on page 99.

Languages Supported	Java

Pure Java repository-driven development environment supporting all the EJB 1.1 roles—Bean provider, Assembler, Deployer, Container, Server, and Administrator.

You can use the Integrated Development Environment—SynerJ Developer, or use any other environment to create EJBs for deployment.

Object Environment

For more information on the object environment, see Chapter 7, "Connecting to Logic: COM, CORBA, EJB, and RMI" starting on page 127.

ORB	CORBA CORBA/IIOP

DCOM
Java/EJB
RMI/IIOP

Component   CORBA
Models   EJB

EJB 1.1 compliant application server supporting EJBs, CORBA, and
CORBA-COM bridge technologies.

Database Environment

The database environment is discussed in Chapter 8, "Connecting to Data: ODBC
and JDBC" starting on page 147.

JDBC

JDBC-based database interaction supporting all popular RDBMS. Provides support for persistent objects (EJB entity beans) and relational
to object mapping techologies.

Transaction Environment

The transaction environment is discussed in Chapter 9, "Transaction Processing and
TP Monitors" starting on page 157.

Java Transaction Service (JTS)

Security Environment

Security is explored in Chapter 10, "Security and Application Servers" starting on
page 173.

SSL 3.0

X.509 Certificates

Security is done declaratively. The actual API calls are generated for the developer.

Interface Environment

See Chapter 6, "Developing the Interface" starting on page 111 for more information on the interface environment.

JSP
XML

Check-box JSP and XML creation. Also additional support for HTML via support for standard HTML authoring products such as Microsoft Frontpage and DreamWeaver.

Other

Management and Development Tools

Includes Application Server monitoring tools that are SNMP compliant. Collects over 200 metrics to manage from the application down to the component.

Provides browser-based as well as script-based administration for unattended operations.

Features

Accelerates Collaborative Development
- Repository-driven component management system

- Collaborative development testing and debugging of code among developers and across machines

- Powerful wizards increase productivity by reducing hand-coding

Integrates Beyond the Java Platform
- Supports multiple component models including CORBA and COM

- XML and IIOP integration adapters

- Adapters to popular application packages and middleware technologies

Scales to Future Demands
- Advanced load-balancing, caching and replication of components

- Supports just-in-time compilers including Sun's HotSpot

Automates Iterative Deployment
- Automatic management of deployment configurations

- Incremental guaranteed code delivery

- Component level reconfiguration without recoding

- Web-based deployment of Java applications and applets

- Zero administration client services

- Flexible HTML client building with the separation of display and business logic

Avoids Vendor Lock-in
- Target deployment to third-party EJB server products

- Import and export of any standard Java source and binary

- Exploit Java2 Enterprise Edition (J2EE)

- Pure EJB1.1 server supporting Entity (Container Managed Persistence) & Session Beans

WEBOBJECTS

Vendor Information

Vendor   Apple Computer, Inc.

URL   http://www.apple.com/webobjects

Contact   Phone (North America): 1-800-879-6398

International phone numbers are listed at:
http://www.apple.com/webobjects/buy.html

Buy online: http://store.apple.com/1-800-795-1000/WebObjects/AppleStore?partNumber=M7165Z/A

Description   WebObjects pioneered the application server market by offering the first comprehensive product in this emerging category. WebObjects provides a flexible, scalable, cross-platform solution to develop and deploy high-performance network applications. It is used by market leading companies to develop compelling e-business solutions, including one-to-one marketing, e-commerce, asset management, and intranet applications.

Production Environment

For more information on the production environment, see Chapter 4, "Sub-Programs and Application Servers" starting on page 85.

Platforms   HP-UX
Mac OS (includes Carbon, etc.)

Solaris
Windows NT

Web Servers   Any CGI supporting Web Server
Apache
Microsoft Internet Information Server
Netscape
Self-contained (no other Web Server)

Connections   CGI
ISAPI
MSAPI
NSAPI

Development Environment

The development environment is discussed in Chapter 5, "Components, Objects, and Application Servers" starting on page 99.

Languages   C
Supported   C++
Java
Objective C

Third-party add-ons include support for other languages including Perl, Python, and Tcl.

Object Environment

For more information on the object environment, see Chapter 7, "Connecting to Logic: COM, CORBA, EJB, and RMI" starting on page 127.

Many object classes and frameworks are provided to handle:
• Request handling and distribution

- HTML generation/parsing
- Component model for reusing HTML interface elements
- Java client interface to server
- Persistent state storage and session management
- Object/entity persistence in data sources

ORB	COM/CORBA/IIOP
	CORBA
	CORBA/IIOP
	DCOM
	Java/EJB
	RMI/IIOP
Component Models	COM/DCOM
	CORBA
	EJB

Database Environment

The database environment is discussed in Chapter 8, "Connecting to Data: ODBC and JDBC" starting on page 147.

DB2
Informix
JDBC
Microsoft
ODBC
Oracle
SQL Server
Sybase

Third-party adaptors support a variety of other databases including OpenBase, Postgres, mySql, FrontBase, PrimeBase, and more.

Transaction Environment

The transaction environment is discussed in Chapter 9, "Transaction Processing and TP Monitors" starting on page 157.

Whatever the HTTP server supports

Security Environment

Security is explored in Chapter 10, "Security and Application Servers" starting on page 173.

LDAP
Whatever the HTTP server supports

Interface Environment

See Chapter 6, "Developing the Interface" starting on page 111 for more information on the interface environment.

XML

To generate HTML dynamically, WebObjects provides a very open architecture for providing using HTML templates that reference external code to generate the dynamic content. That code is kept separate from your HTML files. Again too numerous to count.

Other

Management and Development Tools

Visual Development Tools
- Project Builder: Edit, compile, run, debug environment
- WebObjects Builder: GUI HTML layout application
- Interface Builder: Java client layout application
- EOModeler: Object-relational database mapping tool

Web-based Deployment Tools
- Monitor: Application management and monitoring facilities
- PlaybackManager: Automated testing tool for pre-launch simulation.

Features

Too many to list. Go to http://www.apple.com/webobjects/tech-specs.html for more details. This represents the current shipping version. By the date of this publication of this book, we will have shipped a new version with new features.

WEBSPHERE

WebSphere is a family of products that provides the tools and software for building and deploying Web-based applications for your e-business solutions that can range from simple Web transaction processing to enterprise-wide business applications. These products are built on open, reusable technologies that leverage your existing resources, shorten development cycles, and ease your administration burden. Using open standards and a common, portable programming model, this family of products provides multiple entry points, thereby promoting customer choice and protecting IT investments.

WebSphere Application Server Standard Edition

Vendor Information

Vendor   International Business Machines Corporation

Contact   Paraic Sweeney
                      Vice President, WebSphere Marketing
                      Software Solutions Division
                      IBM Software Group
                      Somers, NY 10589

URL   http://www.ibm.com/software/webservers

Description   IBM WebSphere Application Server Standard Edition, V3.0 is a robust
                      deployment environment for e-business applications. Its components
                      let you build and deploy personalized, dynamic Web content quickly
                      and easily. Using open Java-based technologies and application pro-
                      gramming interfaces (APIs) as well as the latest eXtensible Markup
                      Language (XML) technologies, the Standard Edition lets you leverage
                      your existing resources, shorten development cycles, and ease your
                      administrative burden.

Production Environment

For more information on the production environment, see Chapter 4, "Sub-Programs
and Application Servers" starting on page 85.

Platforms   AIX
                      Solaris
                      Windows NT

Web Servers	Apache
	IBM HTTP Server
	Lotus Domino
	Lotus Domino Go Webserver
	Microsoft Internet Information Server
	Netscape
Connections	ISAPI
	NSAPI

Development Environment

The development environment is discussed in Chapter 5, "Components, Objects, and Application Servers" starting on page 99.

Languages Supported	C
	C++
	Java
	C and C++ are supported via JNI. Also supports Java Script, JSP, NetRexx, XSL/XML.

Object Environment

For more information on the object environment, see Chapter 7, "Connecting to Logic: COM, CORBA, EJB, and RMI" starting on page 127.

ORB	RMI/IIOP
	CORBA and CORBA/IIOP are used internally.
Component Models	None specified

Database Environment

The database environment is discussed in Chapter 8, "Connecting to Data: ODBC and JDBC" starting on page 147.

DB2
JDBC
Oracle

Also supports InstantDB

Transaction Environment

The transaction environment is discussed in Chapter 9, "Transaction Processing and TP Monitors" starting on page 157.

None specified

Security Environment

Security is explored in Chapter 10, "Security and Application Servers" starting on page 173.

LDAP
SSL 3.0
X.509 certificates
Whatever the HTTP server supports

Interface Environment

See Chapter 6, "Developing the Interface" starting on page 111 for more information on the interface environment.

JSP
XML

JSP Multi-Language scripting framework that allows scripting using compilers such as JavaScript, VBscript, Perl, Ticl, NetRexx

---

Other

Management Tools and Development Environment

Site Analyzer, Tivoli Enabled (IDE, site management, etc.)

Features

The Standard Edition, for Web site builders, provides:
• Support for JavaServer Pages, including:

  • Support for specifications .91 and 1.0

  • Extended tagging support for queries and connection management

  • An XML-compliant DTD for JSPs

• Support for the Java servlet 2.1 specification including automatic user session and user state management

• High-speed pooled database access using JDBC for DB2 Universal Database and Oracle

• XML server tools, including a parser and data transformation tools

• A Web site analysis tool for developing traffic measurements to help improve the performance and effectiveness of your Web sites

• Machine translation for dynamic language translation of Web page content

• An IBM HTTP server, including:

  • A new administration GUI

- •Support for LDAP and SNMP connectivity
- Tivoli ready modules
- Additional integration with IBM VisualAge for Java to help reduce development time by allowing developers to remotely test and debug Web-based applications

WEBSPHERE APPLICATION SERVER ADVANCED EDITION

Vendor Information

Vendor   International Business Machines Corporation

Contact   Paraic Sweeney
                Vice President, WebSphere Marketing
                Software Solutions Division
                IBM Software Group
                Somers, NY 10589

URL   http://www.ibm.com/software/webservers

Description   IBM WebSphere Application Server Advanced Edition, V3.0 is a high-performance Enterprise JavaBeans (EJB) server that implements EJB components that incorporate business logic. It supports multiple platforms, databases and transaction systems, providing Java-based gateway and EJB connectivity.

Production Environment

For more information on the production environment, see Chapter 4, "Sub-Programs and Application Servers" starting on page 85.

Platforms	AIX Solaris Windows NT
Web Servers	Apache IBM HTTP Server Lotus Domino Lotus Domino Go Webserver Microsoft Internet Information Server Netscape
Connections	ISAPI NSAPI Connections are internal and are not exposed.

Development Environment

The development environment is discussed in Chapter 5, "Components, Objects, and Application Servers" starting on page 99.

Languages Supported	C C++ Java C and C++ are supported via JNI. Also supports JSP, Java Script, NetRexx, and XSL/XML.

Object Environment

For more information on the object environment, see Chapter 7, "Connecting to Logic: COM, CORBA, EJB, and RMI" starting on page 127.

ORB

CORBA/IIOP
Java/EJB
RMI/IIOP

Component Models

EJB

Database Environment

The database environment is discussed in Chapter 8, "Connecting to Data: ODBC and JDBC" starting on page 147.

DB2
JDBC
Oracle

Transaction Environment

The transaction environment is discussed in Chapter 9, "Transaction Processing and TP Monitors" starting on page 157.

Java Transaction Service (JTS) via EJS
JTA Interfaces for demarketing Transactions

Security Environment

Security is explored in Chapter 10, "Security and Application Servers" starting on page 173.

LDAP
SSL 3.0
X.509 certificates
Whatever the HTTP server supports

Interface Environment

See Chapter 6, "Developing the Interface" starting on page 111 for more information on the interface environment.

JSP
XML

JSP Multi-Language scripting framework that allows scripting using compilers such as JavaScript, VBscript, Perl, Ticl, NetRexx

Other

Management Tools and Development Environment

Site Analyzer, Tivoli Enabled (IDE, site management, etc.)

Features

The Advanced Edition, for Web application programmers, provides all the features of the Standard Edition, plus:
• Full support for the Enterprise JavaBeans (EJB) 1.0 specification

- Deployment support for EJBs, Java servlets, and JSP with performance and scale improvements, including:
  - Applet-level partitioning
  - Load balancing
- Enhanced support for distributed transactions and transaction processing
- Improved management and security controls, including
  - User and group level setup
  - Method level policy and control
- CORBA support, providing both bean-managed and container-managed persistence

WEBSPHERE APPLICATION SERVER ADVANCED EDITION FOR AS/400

Vendor Information

Vendor	International Business Machines Corporation
Contact	Paraic Sweeney Vice President, WebSphere Marketing Software Solutions Division IBM Software Group Somers, NY 10589
URL	http://www.as400.ibm.com/websphere

Description	WebSphere Application Server Advanced Edition for the AS/400 brings to the OS/400 the ability to build active web sites and web applications using Hypertext Markup Language (HTML), Java Servlets and JavaServer Pages (JSPs) just as you can with WebSphere Application Server Standard Edition. In addition, it also supports the Enterprise JavaBeans (EJB) specification from Sun Microsystems. EJB support allows your application to include sophisticated business components that run on the server. These components may include business logic with sophisticated, automatic, distributed transactions, and complex persistence to a relational database.

Production Environment

For more information on the production environment, see Chapter 4, "Sub-Programs and Application Servers" starting on page 85.

Platforms	AS/400
Web Servers	IBM HTTP Server Lotus Domino Any CGI supporting Web server
Connections	CGI ISAPI

Development Environment

The development environment is discussed in Chapter 5, "Components, Objects, and Application Servers" starting on page 99.

Languages Supported	C C++ COBOL

Java
Perl
Smalltalk

Object Environment

For more information on the object environment, see Chapter 7, "Connecting to Logic: COM, CORBA, EJB, and RMI" starting on page 127.

ORB

Java/EJB
RMI/IIOP

Component Models

EJB

Database Environment

The database environment is discussed in Chapter 8, "Connecting to Data: ODBC and JDBC" starting on page 147.

DB2
JDBC

Transaction Environment

The transaction environment is discussed in Chapter 9, "Transaction Processing and TP Monitors" starting on page 157.

EJB

Security Environment

Security is explored in Chapter 10, "Security and Application Servers" starting on page 173.

LDAP
SSL 3.0
X.509 certificates
Whatever the HTTP server supports

Interface Environment

See Chapter 6, "Developing the Interface" starting on page 111 for more information on the interface environment.

JSP
XML

JSP Multi-Language scripting framework that allows scripting using compilers such as JavaScript, VBscript, Perl, Ticl, NetRexx

Other

Management Tools and Development Environment

Site Analysis, VisualAge for Java Enterprise Edition Version 3 (IDE, site management, etc.)

Features

WebSphere Application Server, Advanced Edition enables powerful web transactions and interactions with a robust deployment environment for e-business applications. With a portable, Java-based web application deployment platform focused on supporting and executing

Java servlets, JavaBeans, JavaServer Pages, and Enterprise JavaBeans, this edition interacts with enterprise databases, transaction processing systems, and other applications for dynamic Web content. It builds on the Standard Edition to provide the portability and control of server-side business applications along with the performance and manageability of Enterprise JavaBeans. It extends the value and versatility of this platform with:

• Complete Java and Enterprise Java support, including a server for applications built to the Enterprise JavaBean specification. The focus is on medium- to high-level transactional environments used in conjunction with dynamic Web content generation and Web-initiated transactions.

• Performance and scaling attributes with support for bean-managed and container-managed persistence, for entity beans and session beans, with transaction management and monitoring. Container management and persistent storage helps provide a high-performance transactional environment using servlets and Enterprise JavaBeans.

This WebSphere product is integral to managing and integrating enterprise-wide applications while leveraging open Java-based technologies and APIs. It enables powerful interactions with relational databases, transaction processing systems, and other applications. It is built using CORBA (Common Object Request Broker Architecture) IIOP protocol. This Web application server provides deployment and management of Java and Enterprise JavaBean applications.

Notes

General availability is targeted for first half of 2000. Requires OS/400 V4R4.

WEBSPHERE APPLICATION SERVER ENTERPRISE EDITION

Vendor Information

Vendor   International Business Machines Corporation

Contact   Paraic Sweeney
                  Vice President, WebSphere Marketing
                  Software Solutions Division
                  IBM Software Group
                  Somers, NY 10589

URL   http://www.software.ibm.com/webservers/appserv

Description   IBM WebSphere Application Server Enterprise Edition
                  enables full e-business transactions over the Web. Using open
                  standards-based technologies like interoperable CORBA and Enter-
                  prise JavaBeans (EJBs), Enterprise Edition provides comprehensive,
                  high-quality middleware runtime services for distributed component
                  applications. It also contains the industry's most complete support for
                  integrating existing IT applications and resources for reuse on the
                  Web. This product combines WebSphere Application Server Ad-
                  vanced Edition with the former TXSeries and Component Broker
                  products.

Production Environment

For more information on the production environment, see Chapter 4, "Sub-Programs and Application Servers" starting on page 85.

Platforms   AIX

	OS/390
	Solaris
	Windows NT

Web Servers   Apache
IBM HTTP Server
Lotus Domino
Netscape
Self-contained (no other Web Server)
Microsoft Internet Information Server

For Component Broker: Component Broker supports servlet clients that are Web servers. Conmponent Broker supports downloading Java client code from Web servers, but is not inherently dependent upon one to run.

Connections   ISAPI
NSAPI

For Component Broker: Component Broker is an object server for CORBA- and EJB-based components. We run based on IIOP or RMI/ IIOP listening on a port for inbound requests.

We support servlet clients and clients that are webservers. We support downloading Java client code from webservers, but aren't inherently dependent upon one to run.

Development Environment

The development environment is discussed in Chapter 5, "Components, Objects, and Application Servers" starting on page 99.

Languages
Supported   C
C++
CORBA
Java

Visual Basic

C and C++ are supported via JNI. Also supports JSP, JavaScript, NetRexx, and XSL/XML. Visual Basic is supported only on the client; others are supported on both the client and server.

Object Environment

For more information on the object environment, see Chapter 7, "Connecting to Logic: COM, CORBA, EJB, and RMI" starting on page 127.

ORB

CORBA
CORBA/IIOP
Java/EJB
RMI/IIOP

For TXSeries: TXSeries supports wrappering of TXSeries services as Enterprise JavaBeans. This support uses a CORBA ORB (included). In addition, TXSeries can use ORBIX as a transport layer. The other choice for transport is DCE. TXSeries also supports wrappering of TXSeries services inside COM objects.

*Component
Models*

CORBA

EJB

For TXSeries:
- COM: external wrappering

- EJB: external wrappering

- CORBA: supported

Database Environment

The database environment is discussed in Chapter 8, "Connecting to Data: ODBC and JDBC" starting on page 147.

DB2
JDBC
Oracle

Transaction Environment

The transaction environment is discussed in Chapter 9, "Transaction Processing and TP Monitors" starting on page 157.

CORBA OTS (Open Transaction Standard)
Java Transaction Service (JTS)
JTA Interfaces for demarketing Transactions
X/Open XA and TX

Security Environment

Security is explored in Chapter 10, "Security and Application Servers" starting on page 173.

LDAP
SSL 3.0
X.509 certificates
Whatever the HTTP server supports

For Component Broker: Component Broker supports authentication via SSL and we support CORBA delegation, authentication, and authorization.

Interface Environment

See Chapter 6, "Developing the Interface" starting on page 111 for more information on the interface environment.

JSP

JSP Multi-Language scripting framework that allows scripting using compilers such as JavaScript, VBscript, Perl, Ticl, NetRexx

---

Other

Management Tools and Development Environment

Site Analyzer, Tivoli Enabled

Features

The Enterprise Edition, for Web enterprise architects, includes all the features of the Advanced Edition, plus:

- Full distributed object and business process integration capabilities

- IBM's world-class transactional application environment integration (fromTXSeries)

- Full support for the Enterprise JavaBeans (EJB) 1.0 specification

- Complete object distribution and persistence (from Component Broker)

- Support for MQSeries

- Complete component backup and restore support

- XML-based team development functions

- Integrated Encina application development kit

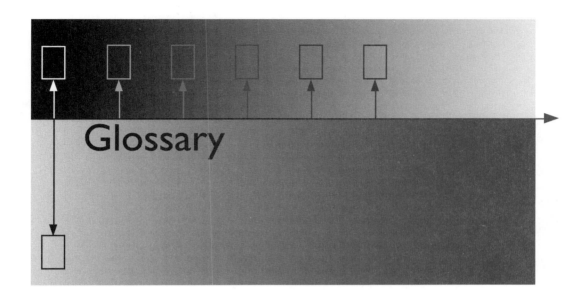

Glossary

24x7
Twenty-four hours a day, seven days a week. Pronounced "twenty-four seven" or "twenty-four by seven." Used in reference to operations that must always be available; 24x7 often connotes attended operation of a system.

Active Server Pages (ASP)
Active Server Pages combine HTML and scripts (in JavaScript, VBScript, or Perlscript). The scripts run on the server and HTML is sent to the client. This Microsoft technology relies on their server products; however, third parties have ported the technology to other environments (such as Unix).

application	A term used to refer to a computer program (as in a "word processing application") or to a process developed for a specific functional purpose (as in "the insurance claim processing application").
API	An application programming interface (API) is the specification of inputs and outputs that allows programmers to write code that interacts with existing software.
bridges	Software (usually custom written) that allows normally incompatible systems and applications to communicate with one another.
browser	Programs such as Netscape Communicator, Microsoft Internet Explorer, or NCSA Mosaic that let you explore the World Wide Web. Proprietary systems such as America Online and private organizations' software may use their own browsers.
business logic	Logic and processing rules specific to a particular organization's work. Business logic is separate from network protocols and logic that applies to all users of a network. It incorporates the organization's policies and procedures.
CRT screens	Cathode Ray Tubes. The devices used to view computer data before flat-panel displays were invented.
data element	An entry in a database structure, such as age, address, or price. Each data element has a name; a data element usually has many values in a database—each value corresponds to one observation, record, or individual.
database	A collection of data that is organized for easy storage and retrieval. Databases are managed by database software such as Oracle or Microsoft Access.
database project	A user-created set of database data that includes data entry screens, documentation, assistance, and reports.
database software	Software that manages databases. Some products are Microsoft Access, DB2, Oracle, Sybase, and FileMaker Pro.

DBMS   Database Management System. Database software.

e-commerce   The use of the Internet for commercial purposes such as buy-
                ing and selling goods and information. E-commerce Web sites
                are often powered by databases.

factoring   The process of separating interface programming from appli-
                cation programming. Factoring is a necessary step in produc-
                ing programs that can be scripted.

FTP   File Transfer Protocol. The Internet protocol used to transfer
                files between computers.

Gopher   The Internet text-based menu system for organizing data.
                Largely replaced by the World Wide Web.

GIF   Graphical Interchange Format. A format (including image
                compression) that is used primarily for computer-generated
                images on the Internet. Compare to JPEG.

hot   Part of a computer image that responds to a mouse click. But-
                tons and links on Web pages are hot.

HTML   HyperText Markup Language. The language used to design
                and format Web pages. If you use a graphical Web page edi-
                tor, you may rarely see raw HTML.

IDE   Integrated Development Environment. A graphically based
                environment that contains a program text editor, compiler,
                linker, and debugger. IDEs allow programmers to switch be-
                tween writing and testing code; often, changes can be made to
                source code while the application is running.

intranet   A network that uses Internet protocols but is not open to the
                general public.

ISP   Internet Service Providers typically provide access to the In-
                ternet: they are the companies at the other end of the phone
                line or cable connection. Internet service providers typically
                offer services in addition to connectivity such as database

hosting, Web-site hosting, e-mail, and so forth. ISPs bundle such services, but many organizations use a variety of vendors to handle the different services.

JPEG
Joint Photographic Experts Group. A compression format for images used on the Web. JPEG is a "lossy" format—each time you save it, part of the image is lost as it is compressed. JPEG is an appropriate format for photographs as opposed to computer-generated images.

MIME
Multipurpose Internet Mail Extension. A format that allows for non-text data to be incorporated into messages.

object-oriented programming
A programming architecture in which small units—objects—are employed. Each object is self-contained, and its interfaces are well-defined. Objects are created (instantiated) as needed and communicate with one another through messages or function calls. In object-oriented programming, global variables and program-wide operations are avoided.

protocols
The rules governing communication between and among hardware and software components.

query
A request to a database for information. Queries may also be used to add information to a database. Today, most queries are formulated using SQL.

record
A given data instance—one student, one shopping order, etc. Each data instance consists of the data values for each of the fields in the table.

RFC
Request for Comments. Internet standards are developed collaboratively within the Internet community. Requests for Comments are issued and input accepted until a standard is set. These standards may later be modified or replaced. RFCs are numbered. For the ultimate word on specific Internet concepts, consult the RFCs. You can find them in many places including www.internic.net; you can also search for "RFC" with a search engine.

scalability	The ability of a system (hardware or software) to be enlarged or decreased in size. Scalability often refers to large changes in size such as going from a Web site that supports 50 transactions a day to one that supports 50,000 transactions a day. Typically, such drastic changes have stressed hardware and software. Desktop software often does not scale up; likewise, enterprise software does not scale down.
Standards Information	Excellent glossaries of terms are available on the Internet. One of the best for telecommunications issues is *Federal Standard 1037C: Glossary of Telecommunications Terms*. It is available at http://ntia.its.bldrdoc.gov/fs-1037/dir-001/_0067.htm.
	W3C—The World Wide Web Consortium develops standards for Web protocols including HTML. You can access W3C at http://www.w3.org/.
	SQL standards can be obtained from the American National Standards Institute at http://web.ansi.org.
	Information about standards and terminology can also be obtained from vendors of specific products.
stateless	Usually used in reference to HTML, stateless refers to the fact that the server does not store information about the client between transmissions. As a result, each message sent to the server must contain all of the data that the server will need to process the transaction.
SQL	Structured Query Language. A common language used to describe and manipulate relational databases.
template file	A file containing part of a Web page. Written in HTML, template files have special elements that enable an application server to merge dynamic information with the prepared HTML in the template.
URL	Uniform Resource Locator. An Internet address.
Web server	A program that provides Web pages on demand to clients. A Web server is assigned a port on a computer; all messages that

come to that computer's port go to the Web server. A Web server may also be the computer that runs a Web server. By using several port numbers, a single Web server computer can run a number of Web server programs.

Webmaster   The person responsible for a Web site.

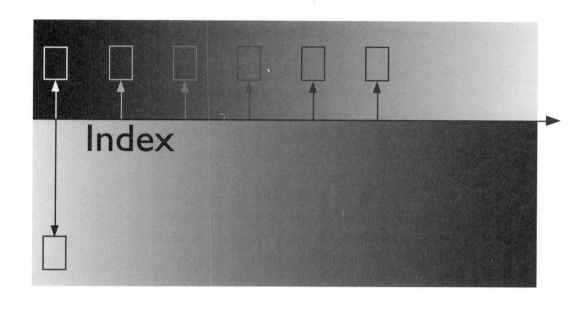

Index

A

Access Control List. *See* ACL
ACL 182
Active Server Pages. *See* ASP
ActiveX controls 113, **118–121**, 124
    marking 119
    signing 119
ActiveX Data Objects. *See* ADO
addressing conventions 12
ADO **151**
APPLET (HTML) 114
applets 88, 113, 124
    Java 116, **121–122**
application
    defined 4
application hosting 26
application layer (TCP/IP)
    security 180

application servers
    and middleware 52
    design of 46–48
    marketplace 51
    origin of 2
    planning for 209
    types of 49–52
        integrated 50
        operating systems 49
        plug-in 50
        standalone 50
    uses for 34–45
application service providers 26
ASP 39, 125
atomicity 160
attribute 9, **68**
authentication
    client 179
    server 179

Principal entries and definitions are shown in **bold**.

B

Berners-Lee, Tim 2
borrowers 175
browsers
    helper applications 89
business logic 196
byte code **88,** 116

C

C 104, 118
C++ 104, 106, 118
CA 181
cardinality **68**
CCITT 181
certificate authority. *See* CA
certificates 181
CFront 106
CGI **95**
chained transactions 162
classes **103**
client authentication 179
client integration 93
client/server
    sub-programs 86
client/server systems 20–21
    Internet-based 21–23
client-side programming 92–93
    client integration 93
    data entry editing 92
    interface enhancement 92
Cobol 104
Cold Fusion 188
column **68**
COM 99, 105, 107, **130–136,** 151, 180
COM/DCOM 118
Common Object Request Broker Architec-
    ture. *See* CORBA
Component Object Model. *See* COM
component technology 102–105
    history of 100–102
    implementation of 106
components
    compared to objects 105
computer age
    history of 2

concurrency 150, 163
connectivity
    non-Internet 26
consistency 160
CORBA 100, 107, 167
    connecting to JavaBeans 124
CORBA Object Transaction Service. *See* OTS
create (SQL) 81
cursors 80

D

data entry editing 92
data link layer (TCP/IP)
    security 178
database drivers 149
    one-tier 149
    three-tier 149
    two-tier 149
Database Management Systems (DBMSs) **57**
database projects **56**
databases 35, **57**
    hierarchic **65**
    inverted list **65**
    network **66**
DCOM **130–136**
declarative programming 76
degree **68**
delete (SQL) 81
dimension **68**
Distributed Transaction Processing. *See* DTP
documentation 194
domain **68**
domain name servers 13
domain name system 13
DTP 166
dumb terminals 19
durability 161

E

e-commerce 43
encryption 179
enterprise computing 26–27
Enterprise JavaBeans 99, 107
eXtensible Markup Language. *See* XML

of end user and productivity tools from vendors including Microsoft, Apple, IBM, and Claris.

He is the author of a number of books including *Database-Driven Web Sites* (Morgan Kaufmann, 1999); *Perl 5 Programmer's Notebook* (Prentice-Hall, 1999); *FileMaker Pro 4 and the World Wide Web* (FileMaker Press, 1999); *Automating FileMaker Pro* (Morgan Kaufmann, 2000); *Cyberdog* (AP Professional, 1996); *ClarisWorks 5.0: The Internet, New Media, and Paperless Documents* (Claris Press, 1998); *Rhapsody Developer's Guide* (AP Professional, 1997); *Essential OpenDoc* (with Anthony Meadow, Addison-Wesley, 1996); and *Real World Apple Guide* (M&T Books, 1995).

Together with Barbara Butler, he wrote *Finding and Fixing Your Year 2000 Problem: A Guide for Small Businesses and Organizations* (AP Professional, 1998; Sybex Verlag, 1999 [German edition], RocketEdition [eBook], 1999). They also wrote *Y2K Bible, Procrastinator's Edition* (IDG Books, 1999). They have spoken, written, and consulted extensively on the Year 2000 problem.

Jesse Feiler serves on the boards of the HB Playwrights Foundation, the Philmont Public Library, and the Mid-Hudson Library System. He is the 1997 recipient of the Velma K. Moore Award given by the New York State Association of Library Boards for "exemplary service and dedication to libraries."

Philmont Software Mill is located on the Web at www.philmontmill.com.